DIGITAL TOOLS IN URBAN SCHOOLS

TECHNOLOGIES OF THE IMAGINATION NEW MEDIA IN EVERYDAY LIFE

Ellen Seiter and Mimi Ito, Series Editors

This book series showcases the best ethnographic research today on engagement with digital and convergent media. Taking up in-depth portraits of different aspects of living and growing up in a media-saturated era, the series takes an innovative approach to the genre of the ethnographic monograph. Through detailed case studies, the books explore practices at the forefront of media change through vivid description analyzed in relation to social, cultural, and historical context. New media practice is embedded in the routines, rituals, and institutions—both public and domestic—of everyday life. The books portray both average and exceptional practices but all grounded in a descriptive frame that renders even exotic practices understandable. Rather than taking media content or technology as determining, the books focus on the productive dimensions of everyday media practice, particularly of children and youth. The emphasis is on how specific communities make meanings in their engagement with convergent media in the context of everyday life, focusing on how media is a site of agency rather than passivity. This ethnographic approach means that the subject matter is accessible and engaging for a curious layperson, as well as providing rich empirical material for an interdisciplinary scholarly community examining new media.

Ellen Seiter is Professor of Critical Studies and Stephen K. Nenno Chair in Television Studies, School of Cinematic Arts, University of Southern California. Her many publications include *The Internet Playground: Children's Access, Entertainment, and Mis-Education; Television and New Media Audiences;* and *Sold Separately: Children and Parents in Consumer Culture.*

Mimi Ito is Professor in Residence and John D. and Catherine T. MacArthur Foundation Chair in Digital Media and Learning, Department of Anthropology and Department of Informatics, University of California, Irvine, and Research Director of the Digital Media and Learning Hub, University of California Humanities Research Institute. She has published widely on new media and youth and led a recently completed three-year project, Kids' Informal Learning with Digital Media, an ethnographic study of digital youth funded by the MacArthur Foundation.

TITLES IN THE SERIES
Skate Life: Re-Imagining White Masculinity by Emily Chivers Yochim
My Life as a Night Elf Priest: An Anthropological Account of World of Warcraft by Bonnie A. Nardi
Home Truths? Video Production and Domestic Life by David Buckingham,
Rebekah Willett, and Maria Pini
Digital Tools in Urban Schools: Mediating a Remix of Learning by Jabari Mahiri

---

DIGITALCULTUREBOOKS, an imprint of the University of Michigan Press, is dedicated to publishing work in new media studies and the emerging field of digital humanities.

DIGITAL TOOLS IN URBAN SCHOOLS

Mediating a Remix of Learning

Jabari Mahiri

THE UNIVERSITY OF MICHIGAN PRESS | ANN ARBOR

Published in the United States of America by
The University of Michigan Press
Manufactured in the United States of America
♾ Printed on acid-free paper

2014   2013   2012   2011   4   3   2   1

A CIP catalog record for this book is available from the British Library.

Library of Congress Cataloging-in-Publication Data

Mahiri, Jabari.
    Digital tools in urban schools : mediating a remix of learning /
Jabari Mahiri.
    p. cm. — (Technologies of the imagination: new media in
everyday life)
    Includes bibliographical references and index.
    ISBN 978-0-472-07153-1 (cloth : alk. paper) — ISBN 978-0-472-05153-3
(pbk. : alk. paper) — ISBN 978-0-472-02760-6
    1. Urban youth—Education—Social aspects—United States.   2. Critical
pedagogy—United States.   3. Digital communications—Social
aspects—United States.   I. Title.
LC5131.M34 2011
371.009173'2—dc22   2011007219

Cover image: Ilja Mašík/Shutterstock

To Helio J. Mahiri ✺ *"the First"*

ACKNOWLEDGMENTS

This book would not have been possible without the vision, passion, and commitment of the principal, teachers, staff, and parents at the high school where this research took place. These inspiring educators and cultural workers are harbingers of the change we need. I also thank their students, whose energy and activities were central to this work. I additionally thank the participants at the University of California, Berkeley, scholar-activists who contributed important perspectives and skills to the TEACH Project: Rick Ayers, Kelly Buchanan, Victor Diaz, Heidi Ku'ulei Hata, Lanette Jimerson, Alexis Martin, Jose Gutierrez, Sonia Martin Poole, Gerald Reyes, Allison Scott, Hillary Scott, Pierre Tchetgen, Sneha Veeragoudar Harrell, and Dawn W. Ferreira. I thank Mersia Gabri El, Casey Hunt, Cherise Martinez-McBride, Roger Smith, Aaron Ward, Joy Lee, Eda Levenson, and Erin Murphy-Graham for their important contributions, as well as Ayesha Walker, Lissa Soep, and Jacinda Abcarian of Youth Radio. Sharon Merritt, Maryanne Berry, and Grace Kim—thanks for our explorations in Second Life. I thank Yvette Jackson, Eric Cooper, LaVerne Flowers, and the other members of the National Urban Alliance who influenced my thinking on working with educators. Also, I thank Mimi Ito, Barrie Thorne, Michael Carter, and the other participants of the Digital Youth Project who provided intellectual community and critical resources for this work. I especially thank members of my family for so much goodness: Kobie Mahiri; Jelani, Nina, and Helio Mahiri; Ayana and Nia Crawford; and Ajamu, Ahlia, and Soleil Kitwana. A special thanks to Miyako Tsujimoto—for everything. Finally, I thank Fani Garagouni, who wonderfully facilitated the research and writing of this book.

CONTENTS

1 | NEW LITERACIES NEED NEW LEARNING

The digital age and the age of hip-hop emerged collaterally during the last 35 years. Increasingly, young people in the United States and globally use screen-based, digital technologies to source and transmit words, images, video, and sounds as they engage in meaning making, identity connections, and social networking. They come to school with experiences, interests, affinities, and skills uniquely enabled by new media, and engaging them in classrooms requires new learning of teachers.

This book reveals significant ways that high school teachers extended their professional learning to revitalize learning in their classrooms in the complex educational context of an urban, public continuation high school in northern California. They did this through participation in a novel professional development project that was part of a university/public school research collaboration called TEACH (Technology, Equity, And Culture in High-performing schools).[1] In this project, teachers were supported and guided in developing perspectives and skills needed to take greater advantage of new media and new information sources in conjunction with relevant connections to youth experiences and interests. This work draws on extensive qualitative data to document, describe, and analyze how the learning of both teachers and students was dramatically transformed as they worked to incorporate an array of new media in their classrooms.

Dewey (1938) argued for an American educational system that respected all sources of experience. So the importance of sourcing experience for learning is not new, but the virtual experiences of digital youth are. The lives and learning of today's young people are permeated with engagements with new media. Consequently, many students come to school with experiences, interests, and skills—different resources for meaning making—that are shaped by and expressed through digital texts and tools. Interestingly, the virtual substance of these affordances often reflects hip-hop cultural influences that are revealed in language, music, images, entertainment media, electronic games, and sports as well as in personal styles and perspectives. Hip-hop's emergence during the global information age vastly increased its reach, and it has had provocative cross-connections with technology and world culture since its inception in the 1970s. For example, rap artists were quickest to exploit digital samplers and sequencers when these and other technologies suited their cultural purposes (Miller 2004). Rose (1994) noted that "hip hop transforms stray technological parts intended for cultural and industrial trash heaps into sources of pleasure and power. These transformations have become a basis of digital imagination all over the world" (22).

Now, through a kind of digital DJ-ing, contemporary youth in the United States and globally utilize technological resources to source, sample, and cut and paste multimedia texts for replay in new configurations, just as hip-hop DJs reconfigure sounds, words, and images to play anew (Mahiri 2006). Digital media allows for greatly increased mobility, interchangeability, and accessibility of all kinds of texts and signs, while it magnifies and simplifies processes for new authorial assemblages, such as multimodal collages and remixes (Gibson 2005; Manovich 2001). It has expanded our notions of textuality and virtuality as well as our sense of space and place. The ubiquitous cell phone is a case in point with its diverse capabilities for accessing written texts, voice recordings, music, pictures, video, TV, the Internet, GPS, clocks, calendars, calculators, and games. Miller (2004) claimed that home is where your cell phone is. Thousands of applications are available for added personalization and performance of smart phones, and many more are continually being developed. These new texts and tools for communication, pleasure, work, and social networking reflect new forms of literacy that offer vast possibilities for meaning making and identity construction for youth and adults (Gee 2003; Johnson 2005; Mahiri 2004b, 2006, 2008). Increasingly, teachers will have to engage the digital imaginations of youth through a new remix of techniques and tools for learning in schools.

Dewey understood seventy years ago that to be effective, teachers needed to change their perspectives as well as their practices. In addition to sourcing experiences, he argued for "the introduction of a new order of conceptions leading to new modes of practice" (1938, 5). Now, new conceptions of design and new practices for delivery of instruction are crucial to education and societal challenges of the twenty-first century. These challenges call for innovative approaches and programs to facilitate teachers in mediating the learning of contemporary youth with appropriate uses of digital technology.

It is important that novel approaches to teaching and learning with technology were able to take place in the challenging setting of an urban, continuation high school. Continuation high schools are distinguished from other kinds of schooling alternatives to traditional high schools in that students are assigned to and required to attend continuation schools against their wills, often for severe discipline problems or chronic under-achievement. Students can be sent to continuation high schools based on these issues at any time during the school year, and they later may be allowed to return to the main school. Continuation schools are some-times pejoratively referred to as "dumping grounds" or "pre-prisons." Village Tech High (V-Tech),[2] however, was a continuation school that was already taking a different approach to teaching its "involuntary" students that included expectations of academic rigor, the selection of caring and committed faculty and staff members, and the creation of partnerships with community and other institutional resources. Its col-laboration in the TEACH Project to increase the effectiveness of profes-sional development for its teachers was seen by the school community as complementary to other efforts being taken at the school.

Ms. Glide,[3] an African American woman who was new to the teach-ing profession and also a new teacher at V-Tech, reflected the dilemma of many educators. "I completely resisted the idea of integrating technology into my practice," she wrote in response to an interview question about her early teaching. She further noted, "My feelings stemmed primarily from my limited technological proficiency and the related fear of trying to teach things to students that I didn't understand myself." Part of the dilemma is that young people often have more expansive experiences with digital media than their teachers. Most students—including those who are underperforming in school—extensively use cell phones, text messaging, YouTube, and Twitter; they are avid downloaders of digital music; they are comfortable with basic Internet searching; they use digi-tal photography and video and play an array of video games. Many have blogs and Facebook or Myspace pages and profiles. As Alvermann (2008) noted, young people come to school with different technological experi-ences in contrast to older generations that are not addressed by instruc-tion. Still, the value of these digital practices of youth is often contested or seen in opposition to traditional literacies surrounding page-based texts (Rich 2008). This issue will be addressed later in this chapter. Yet, as Lankshear and Knobel (2002) have argued, page-based texts and their corresponding instructional practices do not compete well in what they called the "attention economy." As one student noted, "When I come to school, I feel like I have to power down." Powering down, or the sense of a loss of power, is even more pronounced for underachieving students who are pushed to the margins of schooling through academic disengagement and disciplinary problems (Gregory, Nygreen, and Moran 2006).

Discussions and critiques of the problems of urban, public schools in the United States are pervasive, particularly with regard to their failures with underachieving students like those assigned to V-Tech.[4] One major aspect of school failure in this country is the rising rate of dropouts with its disparate economic, social, and health consequences for those who do not complete high school (McNeil et al. 2008). According to the National Center for Education Statistics, negative outcomes from dropping out of high school include significantly lower annual incomes ($20,000 versus nearly $30,000 for graduates), much higher unemployment rates, worse health conditions as adults, and far greater possibilities of going to prison and of being on death row (Laird et al. 2007). The research of Balfanz and Legters (2004) indicated how dropping out is increasingly a problem of urban schools and particular regions of the country. They found, for example, that nearly 80 percent of high schools with the highest dropout rates are in just 15 states, and California is one of these (vi).

Recent work revealing more accurate tracking systems for high school dropouts in California suggests that school failure with regard to this factor is significantly worse than generally assumed. With the new student tracking system, school officials determined that the projected dropout rate for African American students in the state—the most extreme example—was an astronomical 42 percent, approximately twice as high as earlier claims using the old system (Asimov 2008). Another important aspect of educational decline is the breakdown in the pipeline between this nation's high schools and its colleges and universities. Within the last decade, after having pioneered mass higher education, the United States has gone from first to fourteenth among nations in the world in rates of participation in postsecondary education. The United States currently ranks twenty-first in high school graduation rates, and Europe is now the first choice of international students (Douglass 2008). In significant ways with regard both to national and global contexts, this country's schools are also failing many of its highest achieving students.

Questions are now being raised as to whether schools can be saved or are worth saving. For example, in a speech in 2005 to the National Governors Association, Bill Gates, whose education philanthropy has been immense, claimed that this country's high schools are obsolete. He went on to say that even when schools are "working exactly as designed . . . [they] cannot teach our kids what they need to know today" ("American high school" 2006, 12). In this milieu, major private funding (and some government) agencies are consciously shifting their focus and resources from school reform initiatives to what they consider to be more promising venues of youth informal learning, or to innovative literacy programs taking place after school. In line with this, formulations by groups like the Economic Policy Institute suggest that schools alone cannot combat the broad social factors that contribute to failing schools, so more money should go to health care programs, antipoverty initiatives, and after-school and pre-K programs. Groups like the Education Equality Project agree that focusing on these kinds of programs and initiatives is important, but they also argue that reforms that change the fundamental structure and accountability systems of schools can make a big difference (Brooks 2008).

In light of these considerations, I am not arguing that increasing the use of technology for learning is a panacea for failing schools. Clearly, political, socioeconomic, cultural-historical, and geographic factors—like priorities for government spending, the growing divide between rich and poor, intense global competition and changing markets, and the increasing role of standardized testing—are intricately linked to problematic outcomes in our schools. However, school structures that result in disproportionate numbers of inexperienced teachers being assigned to teach in high-poverty schools or with the lowest-performing students in comprehensive schools are one of the problems that sorely needs to change. This problem is dramatically documented in a report by the National Commission on Teaching and America's Future (Carroll et al. 2004). Similarly, an analysis of recent Education Trust data that utilized a highly refined Teacher Quality Index (Carey 2007) identified many subtle and overt ways that students who face the greatest educational challenges receive much less opportunity to be taught by the most qualified teachers. At the same time, reviews of research summarizing hundreds of studies over several decades have shown that better preparation of teachers is a direct way to transform schooling and increase student achievement (Darling-Hammond 1997, 2000). Consequently, the TEACH Project focused its work on the professional development of teachers as a key lever for school change.

A critical challenge for teacher preparation and professional development programs, however, is to enable teachers to understand and utilize relevant digital technologies that can be viable resources for learning. In the spring of 2008, Ms. Glide completed a master's degree along with a secondary English teaching credential from a university whose school of education is ranked in the top 10 in the country. Yet there was very little in her preparation at the university and in her professional development while working in schools that helped her to teach with new technology. What she did get in her preparation program had to do more with learning about technology than with ways of using technology to learn. During her initial interview for the research project she noted, "As a new teacher, I wanted to simplify rather than complicate my teaching. I viewed technology as an inconsistent, logistical nightmare replete with malfunctioning programs and equipment—sure to end in frustration for teacher and students alike." Based on considerable work in professional development with over 25 school districts across the country during the past six years as a senior scholar for the National Urban Alliance for Effective Education (NUA), it is clear to me that this view is also held by many practicing teachers. I have addressed this issue in terms of new considerations for teaching practices in a number of earlier books and journal articles.[5] That this view on teaching with technology could be held by young, promising, new teachers as well as highly experienced teachers was one of the compelling reasons I initiated the TEACH Project to collaboratively deploy research and resources at the university and school district levels to redesign programs of teacher professional development.

Why haven't teacher preparation and teaching practices changed in conjunction with dramatic changes in technology? With all the recent work being done to certify and professionalize teachers, something remains amiss regarding their general lack of facility with technology. Stigler and Hiebert (1999) claimed that despite the continuous succession of reform initiatives, the system and culture of schooling in the United States essentially reproduce teachers who teach pretty much the way that they have been taught. From their comparative analysis of Japanese, German, and U.S. teaching, they argued that many more opportunities were needed for teachers to learn on the job, particularly with and from other teachers, if they were going to improve significantly as professionals. For new knowledge and skills to be acquired and effectively implemented, they concluded, teachers need to have both the time and support to systematically and collaboratively study and work to improve their teaching practices.

These and other perspectives that will be further delineated later in this chapter were key to the formulation and implementation of the TEACH Project. For several reasons that will also be discussed, the school site for the project was primed for a new approach to professional development to transform teaching and learning. Essentially, it provided an educational context that allowed project participants to engage in as well as study the processes of learning and teaching with digital technologies. Describing these processes provides insights into how other school contexts may also be transformed. The implications are not just for underachieving urban schools but for schooling generally in the United States. In her first interview for the TEACH Project, Ms. Glide echoed the feelings of many teachers when she said, "I failed to see how technology could be a useful tool in my practice without me submitting to painful, substantial, intensive instruction." This book chronicles how she and her colleagues worked together with university-based educators to ameliorate this perspective in order to bring a new and more effective remix of learning to their school.

THE TEACH PROJECT

I am the principal investigator of the TEACH Project. It works collaboratively with teachers to support and guide them in rethinking their design and retooling their delivery of instruction in order to more effectively build on and extend the learning, academic achievement, and social development of their students. Ms. Glide ultimately was a self-described technophobe, but in her final interview for the project, she recounted how this collaborative effort changed her perspective on teaching. "Workshops on software programs and unit plan development helped teachers reconsider the ways that multimedia can address student modalities and interests," she noted. "I have found that the workshops have assuaged my initial fears of technology and allowed me to be more imaginative."

Two main goals framed the work of the TEACH Project during the 2007–8 school year that is the focus of this book. The first goal was to develop and document an approach to teacher professional development that integrated effective principles of teaching with successful strategies for mediating student learning with digital media. The second goal was to collaborate with, coach, and support teachers to implement and refine the knowledge and skills learned in this project as core augmentations of their teaching practices, perspectives, and curriculum. Documenting this project included descriptions of the conceptual frameworks, professional development approaches, and teaching and learning activities and products connected to its implementation, along with an assessment of its general feasibility in other educational settings. Three central research questions that guided the project were specifically how the teachers could learn to change their practices in order to more effectively mediate student learning—particularly with digital technologies; what key obstacles and challenges might be encountered in changing teaching and learning through incorporating more technology; and what key changes in the process and products of students' learning could be connected to changing teacher practices.

Beginning in the summer before and continuing through the 2007–8 school year, a team of faculty and student researchers at the University of California, Berkeley,[6] under my direction worked in collaboration with faculty, administrators, and community members at V-Tech. The school's new principal, who was in his third year, had changed the traditional name of the school and advocated for a technology orientation as part of his efforts to move beyond the stigma of a continuation high school. He was also the first principal in the more than 30-year history of the school to develop a curriculum that made it possible for students to fulfill minimum college requirements before graduation. His continuing efforts to transform the school were key to the viability of this collaborative effort.

My initial connection to this school began in the spring of 2003, when I was invited to be the speaker for its graduating class. One thing that was obvious was that the vast majority of the students at this school were African American. I had worked on a long-term research project with the comprehensive high school that sent its "problem" students to this continuation high school, and I kept informed of events and issues at the school. In 2006, two graduate students in my urban education class were also doing their educational psychology field placements at the school. I talked with them often, and it became clear through their excitement that the school was undergoing dramatic changes under the leadership of the new principal. He had a master's degree in educational technology, and his vision was to go beyond support and care for these students and provide them with a challenging curriculum that could significantly change their perspectives and possibilities regarding learning and work in and beyond school. The "three R's" of education for the school became "relationships," "rigor," and "relevance." He selected faculty and staff members, generally younger professionals, who supported the need for healthy relationships with students as well as family and community members who wanted to work toward the new mission for the school to provide both rigorous, college-preparatory, academic work and preparation for jobs that were relevant to the students' communities and personal experiences.

When the principal began work at the school, the Academic Performance Index (API) rating was a mere 317. The API is a numeric index (or scale) ranging from a low of 200 to a high of 1,000 that reflects a school's performance level based on the results of statewide testing. The performance target for all California schools is 800. After the first year of work by the principal, the API score for the school went up significantly; it then went down slightly after his second year. After his third year, the 2007–8 academic year, during which the TEACH Project was implemented, the school's API score jumped from 429 to 586, the highest increase of any school in its county. This score actually surpassed the 574 API rating of the African American students at the comprehensive high school that sends students to V-Tech because they are underachieving and/or designated as severe discipline problems.

Interestingly, in the 2007–8 school year, there was not a single fight at V-Tech. However, this is not to say that there were not serious problems at the school. In the spring of 2008, there was a major theft of 10 laptop computers from the school's mobile computer lab. Also during that spring, one V-Tech student shot a classmate in a neighborhood away from the school site, and another V-Tech student was also shot and killed in neighborhood violence. Violence is clearly a prevalent force in most of these students' lives. In reviewing student records, the school's counselors have noted that they can almost always trace the root of academic and discipline problems back to one or more major traumatic events that these students have experienced.

Most of the students who come to the school read and write well below grade level, and their overall academic skills vary greatly. In addition to behavioral considerations, some have substance abuse issues.

Throughout the academic year of our collaboration, all of the teachers struggled with inconsistent student attendance in their classes. For example, in her second interview Ms. Glide noted, regarding her World Media classes that are the focus of chapter 4: "There are 22 students on the roster [in each class], but rarely more than 15 in attendance on a given day. The total number of students present does not reflect the fact that the class often contains a different grouping of students each day." An important perspective at the school, however, was not to essentialize these youths. Instead, V-Tech's principal, teachers, and staff have consciously worked toward a perspective that is reflective of the view of prominent scholars of African American education that "black youth [are] diverse human beings engaged in normal developmental tasks under difficult conditions" (Spencer 2008, 253). Consequently, educators must always be aware of how differences both inside groups and between groups are dynamically constructed and positioned within historical, political, socioeconomic, and geographic contexts.

The V-Tech campus is about a mile away from the comprehensive high school. It is a small school with nine classrooms, one computer lab, and a modest library space. The staff offices, a multipurpose room, and the library are located in separate buildings at the front of the school. There are two rows of portable classrooms situated in the back of the school facing a small, elongated grassy area. A building in back of the school is occupied by the comprehensive high school's Independent Study program, and it is separated from the rest of the campus by a tall metal fence. V-Tech has student-created artwork and tile murals throughout the campus that provide a colorful, pop-culture aesthetic.

The school has a faculty of 10 teachers (8 of whom participated in the project),[7] and a maximum capacity of 150 students. New students arrive at the school nearly every week of the academic year. The demographic makeup of the comprehensive high school is approximately 30 percent White, 30 percent African American, 17 percent Latino, 8 percent Asian, and 15 percent multiracial. All of the students in the Independent Study program on the other side of the fence are white. By contrast, the students at V-Tech are approximately 85 percent African American and 15 percent Latino. They are also 65 percent male, and 100 percent qualify for free lunch. Thirty-four percent qualify for special education services. Although many of these students eventually have the option to return to the comprehensive high school, approximately 90 percent decide to stay at V-Tech.

Data for this book comes from a range of qualitatively documented activities of the TEACH Project. The school's principal worked extensively with the university team to design and implement 90-minute professional development (PD) sessions for all of the school's teachers, although two were not able to participate. These sessions occurred approximately every other week for the duration of the 2007–8 school year. They operated recursively in facilitating teachers to develop and implement lesson plans in their content areas that incorporated things like podcasting, blogs, digital photography and video, Google Maps, GarageBand, and Teen Second Life. Teachers gained skill and comfort with a specific digital tool in each session, experimented with some level of its deployment in their instruction during the following week(s), and then shared and critiqued their teaching experience in using the tool with other teachers and project participants in subsequent PD sessions.

With continual collaboration of the TEACH team, I guided the PD sessions during the first semester, and a member of the project who has significant technological expertise guided the sessions during the second semester. All of the PD sessions were recorded as well as documented with field notes. Key additional sources of data came from our observations and field notes on teaching and learning connected to the PD in selected teachers' classrooms. Surveys and interviews of the teachers were conducted at the beginning and end of the school year to capture prior and emerging approaches and perspectives on teaching and learning and to develop profiles of their professional and educational backgrounds. The principal was also interviewed at the beginning and end of the school year. Teacher-written narratives and reflections on their experiences with learning and implementing elements from the professional development were collected during and at the end of the school year. Student reflections on their classroom activities connected to the project were also noted during classroom observations. Additionally, members of the research team wrote reflective and analysis notes to capture specific vantage points that they had on the PD activities. Finally, the digital affordances of many of the PD activities allowed for considerable documentation of the teachers' work and learning on a PD website and in teacher-created blogs, podcasts, and other digital media. So the data for this research was generated from the eight V-Tech teachers and their principal who formally consented to take part in this project with the understanding that pseudonyms would be used to conceal real identities in the publication of this work. Elements of the teaching and learning in the classes of two of these teachers were also brought into focus through observations in some of their classes that were documented mainly with field notes.

These data were used to address the three central research questions of the TEACH Project, already identified at the beginning of this section. The primary discussion of how teachers learned to use digital tools to change their practices has been presented in chapter 3 through extensive description and analysis of the work that all the participating teachers did in the PD sessions throughout the academic year. Description and analysis of the nature and products of the students' learning as well as obstacles encountered have been presented in chapter-length discussions of the work of two focal teachers out of the eight who participated in the project. Ms. Foster was one of the most experienced teachers in the school, and she eventually incorporated more technology into her instruction than any other teacher. I focus on her Hip-Hop Journalism class in chapter 2 to provide compelling examples of the range and possibilities (as well as some of the obstacles) for mediating teaching and learning with digital tools in this school setting. Ms. Glide was the least experienced participating teacher, and yet, by the second semester, she was willing to engage her students in learning in Teen Second Life, an online, multi-user virtual environment (MUVE), with the support of members of the TEACH team. In chapter 4, I focus on the work with this unit in her World Media class to provide interesting examples of the real learning that can take place in virtual worlds. In chapter 5, I provide concluding considerations of the teachers' and students' learning along with implications for wider settings of schooling.

My approach in this book was to develop a narrative quality to the presentation of the data in each of the three descriptive/analysis chapters (chapters 2–4), to make the work more accessible to teachers, other educational practitioners, and general readers, in addition to researchers. Rather than citing each interview, survey, written reflection, or field note used as a source for the comments and activities described, I worked toward a dialogic quality, so that the scenes in the PD sessions and in the classrooms unfold as a kind of story that attempts to connect what selected teachers were learning and doing in professional development with how learning was being mediated with students in selected classrooms.

Essentially, V-Tech provided something of a laboratory in which to try new conceptions and new practices of teaching. My perspectives on teacher professional development have been substantially influenced by my ongoing research in urban public schools; by my years of teaching in the Multicultural Urban Secondary English Master's and Credential Program at the University of California, Berkeley; and by the NUA's extensive work in this area in over 25 major urban school districts throughout the country. I have worked with NUA as a senior scholar presenting my research in many of these school districts since 2003. This national organization has developed comprehensive frameworks and many effective teaching strategies that facilitate teachers achieving "high intellectual performances" with increasing numbers of their students. My experiences working with NUA have contributed to my understanding of what is needed for successful professional development of teachers.

In the TEACH Project specifically, our central focus on teachers learning to rethink and retool their instruction became part of an emerging theory of change that was collaboratively developed to provide guides and goals for our work at the school. This approach incorporated a dynamic remix of key pedagogical perspectives in order to provide a multifaceted conceptual framework for effective teaching with technology. For its documented success in guiding teacher effectiveness across disciplines, we drew on the five standards of effective pedagogy developed by the Center for Research in Education, Diversity, and Excellence (CREDE) (Tharp et al. 2001). I felt that these standards were also consistent with core NUA strategies. Additionally, we drew on the four principles of the "pedagogy of collegiality" developed by Chavez and Soep (2005), because of their effectiveness in guiding the learning of urban youth with new media at Youth Radio International, a highly successful youth development organization. Finally, we drew on 6 of the 36 principles of learning with new media that have been defined and articulated by Gee (2004), and all of these perspectives were directed toward being realized through project-based learning. The integration of these perspectives can be imagined as a platform for supporting project-based learning that has three legs: the CREDE standards, the pedagogy of collegiality, and Gee's (2004) new media learning principles. In this image, CREDE's role for "activity centers" would be the seat of this platform.

CREDE's standards are (1) joint productive activity among teachers and students; (2) language and literacy development across academic disciplines; (3) connecting academic content to students' prior knowledge and experiences; (4) using challenging, complex tasks for learning; and (5) engaging students in planned, goal-directed dialogues called instructional conversations (Tharp et al. 2001). CREDE feels that the use of "activity centers" is important for fully realizing these principles in classroom instruction. The pedagogy of collegiality that undergirds Youth Radio's acclaimed programs and pioneering strategies for effective digital learning of youth is a powerful way of reconceiving youth and adult participation in teaching and learning. Its features are (1) joint framing of media projects, (2) youth-led inquiry as a key form of learning, (3) mediated intervention to incorporate comprehensive perspectives into the inquiry and to increase the possibility of influencing social change, and (4) distributed accountability between all participants in the production of media projects (Chavez and Soep 2005).

From the 36 principles of learning connected to new media that are outlined by Gee (2004), we focused on the multimodal, the semiotic, the material intelligence, the distributed, the probing, and the active, critical learning principles. These principles are defined and discussed later in this chapter in the section "What's New about New Literacies." All of these approaches supported the enactment of project-based learning that had the elements of "prompt," "process," "product," "presentation," and "reflection" as a systematic cycle for learning, including digitally mediated learning. Although there have been important successes with urban students in some after-school programs (Chung 2000; C. S. Mott Foundation 2005), students should also be able to consistently experience dynamic, culturally connected, digitally mediated learning during the six or more hours a day that they spend in school. The combination of principles and perspectives we enacted at V-Tech framed our work to achieve this goal.

SUMMARY OF THIS BOOK'S CONTENTS

The four following chapters describe and assess the TEACH approach and how it worked in and beyond the PD sessions in guiding and supporting teachers to change their perspectives and practices in the use of digital tools. As noted earlier, chapter 2 looks at enactments of elements of this approach in Ms. Foster's classroom. Through the teaching and learning activities described, we also get an initial view of V-Tech students learning with new media. Ms. Foster was hired at the beginning of the 2007–8 school year, and because she was a veteran, credentialed teacher with more experience than most of the other teachers, the principal and I asked her to informally take the lead in piloting some aspects of the TEACH Project in her classroom. She selected to do this primarily with an elective class that she offered, Hip-Hop Journalism. She gave the class this title to signal that the curriculum would address issues that were important to contemporary youth from the perspective of investigative journalism. In this class, she placed considerable emphasis on digital mediation of student learning and on incorporating some of the successful strategies for working with young people that are used at Youth Radio. The principal and the TEACH Project supported Ms. Foster in bringing in a collaborator from Youth Radio, Ms. Young, to also work with this class.

With the context of teaching and learning at V-Tech partially reflected through descriptions of the activities in Ms. Foster's class, chapter 3 presents the project's specific work that took place in the actual PD sessions with the eight participating teachers. Research has shown that there is no real value in incorporating technology into teaching just for technology's sake (Alvermann 2008). Effective teaching is a complex process that requires abilities and skills to simultaneously perform a wide range of intricate, interrelated tasks to prompt, mediate, and assess student learning. The teachers and administrators had already done a number of important things to change the culture of the school to one of caring consistent with its "three R's" of "relationships," "rigor," and "relevance." But the principal also noted how a number of the students would say that though they could see the teachers and staff really cared about them, their actual learning was not significantly different from what they had received at the comprehensive high school. In addition to caring, the students needed a more dynamic process of learning.

Chapter 3 describes the early work of the project to provide a common vision and language for teaching and learning, framed initially by CREDE principles, in conjunction with our specific approach to project-based learning, and also by considerations for a collegial pedagogy in conjunction with principles of learning with new media. The chapter documents the ways that teachers were learning to incorporate these perspectives into instruction across the disciplines. It also describes how the teachers themselves moved from novice to more expert users of a variety of digital tools, and it illustrates the importance of the teachers' disciplinary knowledge with respect to the effective use of these tools. Additionally, the chapter shows how the learning of the teachers in the PD sessions was designed to model approaches that they also could use to engage their students' learning in classrooms. Essentially, this chapter chronicles what was productive and problematic in the process of the project's participants developing as "digital teachers."

Chapter 4 looks at an enactment of digitally mediated teaching and learning in the class of a new teacher, Ms. Glide, who was in her first year of teaching. She was motivated by the school's renewed focus on meaningfully incorporating more technology into instruction and wanted to get past her apprehension of making significant changes in her instructional approach. The chapter focuses on two classes she taught during the spring semester of 2008 in the language arts curriculum, entitled World Media. These classes had a thematic focus on global issues and personal awareness. The discussion in the chapter is primarily of a two-week unit in which Ms. Glide (supported by the TEACH Project) guided her students on explorations and learning in the MUVE called Teen Second Life. We extensively documented the activities surrounding this unit from a number of vantage points of the various participants. The digital media itself offered each participant novel ways to capture and preserve audio, visual, and written texts of each activity. It was an important project for understanding the directions that digitally mediated learning might take. Moving from our familiar world to explorations of life and learning in a virtual world took Ms. Glide and her students to frontiers that, as of yet, have little mapping. The chapter charts and critiques their journeys into this new and fertile, virtual terrain.

The final chapter synthesizes the findings of these digital and virtual explorations in terms of their implications for schooling. It provides a concluding assessment of the project's work to change the perspectives and practices of teachers at V-Tech in order to ameliorate academic outcomes for their students. It attempts to shed light on the pivotal question, raised by some of the school's students, of what the term *Tech* in the school's name really means relative to approaches to teaching and learning that are different from the typical practices that have pushed them to the margins of school. Although this work was with teachers of underachieving students, this chapter provides implications for much wider school settings. A fundamental consideration from this work is that with ever-expanding modes for making meaning effective teachers are even more crucial. This chapter presents these implications as initial indications of how the structure and culture of U.S. schools might be changed, in part through incorporating appropriate technology, to vitalize learning and make it relevant to the challenges of a new century.

WHAT'S NEW ABOUT NEW LITERACIES

Many scholarly works explore the emergence and functions of new literacies, and in this section, I use this scholarship to illuminate ways that contemporary teaching needs to change. The sociocultural turn in understanding literacy pivots on a core concept in New Literacy Studies—that reading, writing, and meaning are always situated in specific social practices within specific discourses (Gee 1990). Street's (1984) earlier research and development of the idea of "literacy practices" to refer to both behavior and conceptualizations related to reading and writing helped to seed expanding notions of literacies as always being embedded in broader cultural practices—rather than having independent value—and patterned by social and historical contexts and institutions. Literacy practices, then, are shaped by social rules that work to regulate the use, distribution, production, and significance of written texts (Barton and Hamilton 2000), and the habitus of institutions of schooling plays key roles in determining these processes (Bourdieu and Passeron 1977).

What is new about new literacies is that the nature of texts as well as the materials and processes of text production and distribution are dramatically transformed by digital technology. This changes the social rules surrounding literacy practices as well as the social roles (or functions) these practices play. A characteristic of these changes, in part, is a movement from page to screen. Print texts are ever prominent, but other textual mediums are increasingly available for meaning making, mediums that are highly accessible, interactive, portable, and interchangeable. These qualities result from digital media's capabilities to incorporate graphics, moving images, sounds, shapes, and other forms of texts into computable data (Manovich 2001). Essentially, new media enables new literacies.

A number of scholars have argued that computer games can provide highly viable designs for productive learning of youth (Gee 2004; Johnson 2005; Shaffer 2006; Shaffer et al. 2005). In exploring learning and literacy associated with video games, for example, Gee (2004) defined 36 learning principles connected to digital media. A number of these principles were useful in illuminating the learning that took place with teachers in the PD sessions and with students in their classrooms. The vision of V-Tech's principal was ultimately to utilize the best principles from video games in the design of all learning at the school. The professional development did not attempt to go that far. However, in the sessions, we did place considerable focus on six of the principles outlined by Gee that we found to be highly interrelated and intricately connected to new literacies.

We explored implications for learning for the *multimodal principle* (how meaning and knowledge are built up through various modalities, not just words) in conjunction with the *semiotic principle* (that learning involves interrelations with and across multiple, complex sign systems). Similarly, we explored implications for the *material intelligence principle* (that thinking, problem solving, and knowledge can be designed into and stored in material objects). Another important principle for our formulations that extends considerations of material intelligence is the *distributed principle* (that meaning and knowledge are distributed across the learner, objects, tools, symbols, technologies, and the environment). This principle accommodates a collective intelligence, the networking that allows the access of knowledge from other people, texts, and tools that is enabled by communicative technologies. We felt that these four principles facilitated learning that is often reflected by the *probing principle* (that learning is a cycle of probing and continually reflecting in and on this action) and that they were directly realized through the *active, critical learning principle* (that the learning environment created by these principles encourages active and critical, rather than passive, learning). In assessing the actual learning in conjunction with the incorporation of technology into instruction, it became clear that a number of other principles outlined by Gee (2004) were also in play, and ways that they were reflected in the learning of teachers and students are discussed in subsequent chapters.

In continuing Gee's work on computer games, Shaffer (2006) noted that it is these new ways of learning and new ways of thinking about learning, rather than computers and video games themselves, that should be the focus for parents, educators, and policy makers. He noted that preparation for a world with increasing emphasis on creative thinking requires young people to learn the epistemologies that underlie the work of innovative professionals. He proposed the use of *epistemic games*—games that are fundamentally about learning to think innovatively—as a key way to do this. But he felt that these kinds of games are different from school, and he focused on how they could be played in out-of-school settings like clubs, after-school programs, summer camps, and community centers. He claimed that "schools as currently organized make it difficult to prepare kids for innovation through epistemic games" (182).

Scholarship on technology and learning in urban contexts is often focused on settings beyond school. Recent articles on the concept of collegial pedagogy (Chavez and Soep 2005; Chavez, Turalba, and Malik 2006), on community-based media production (Fleetwood 2005; Poyntz 2006; Soep 2006; Charmaraman 2008), on cultural considerations of learning in digital environments (Gutiérrez 2002; Lee 2005), on structures of participation in digital culture (Ito 2007; Boyd 2007), and on digital storytelling projects (Davis 2005; Hull and Katz 2006) provide insights on digital mediation of learning and literacy with youth in nonschool settings. Additionally, there are a number of recent books that, like these articles, explore voluntary, informal digital learning and experiences of youth outside of schools (Alvermann 2002; Gee 2004; Goodman 2003; Gruber 2000; Hill and Vasudevan 2008; Johnson 2005; McLaren et al. 1995; Shaffer 2006; Tompkins 2006; Willoughby and Wood 2008).

In looking at school contexts specifically, there are some works that offer insights into various school contexts where technology is used to enhance learning (Mahiri 2006; Warschauer 2006). Generally, research on technology in science education seems to be ahead of work on other school subjects or work that goes across school disciplines. For example, early "think papers" of Halverson and Gomez (1998) and others associated with the Center for Learning Technologies in Urban Schools, funded by the National Science Foundation, examined possibilities and paradoxes of technological innovation in partnership with public school systems of Chicago and Detroit. Books by Linn and Hsi (2000) and Linn and Davis (2004) on computers, teachers, and peers as learning partners and on affordances of Internet environments for learning look at schooling but with a focus on science education. Clearly, more research in other school subjects as well as work that goes across school disciplines is needed to illustrate how schooling can and must change to incorporate viable uses of technology.

MEDIATING A REMIX OF LEARNING

This book uniquely contributes to understanding the possibilities and challenges of incorporating technology into schooling through descriptions and analyses of the sustained work of V-Tech teachers and students learning with new media. In attempting to apprehend the pedagogical implications of "what's new about new literacies," the TEACH Project proposed and sought to realize two key conceptual turns. The first was a turn for teachers away from being deliverers of instruction to conceiving of themselves (and ultimately becoming) "mediators" of student learning. The second was a turn for teachers to "remix" student learning with an array of digital texts and tools in order to increase their engagement, achievement, and personal/social development. In mediating a remix of learning with digital media, the teachers worked to enact the principles that were incorporated into the TEACH approach and particularly to understand and leverage both the material intelligence and the collective intelligence available to extend student learning. The following chapters describe how these turns occurred at V-Tech. The remainder of this chapter gives rationales for these turns in terms of what teachers would actually be doing while "mediating a remix of learning" and why this is significant for transforming teaching and learning in schools.

The structure and culture of schooling in the United States reproduce teaching practices that resist change, and these practices are sustained by a system and philosophy of hierarchical organization of ideas, institutions, and individuals. Deleuze and Guattari (1987) noted that these kinds of Western systems are reflected metaphorically in a "tree" image: "The Tree or Root as an image, endlessly develops the law of the One that becomes two, then of the two that become four. . . . Binary logic is the spiritual reality of the root-tree" (5). Essentially, Western imaginations are rooted in the play of hierarchies and dualisms like right and wrong, smart and dumb, work and play, teachers and students. Deleuze and Guattari argued for the necessity of shifting to an alternate metaphorical frame, that of the "rhizome," in which the tree is supplanted by the image of a subterranean stem or bulb. The roots of this orientational frame are revealed in a multiplicity of access points and connectivities, like a rhizome system of underground stems and tubers. They noted that two of the key principles of this system are "connection and heterogeneity: any point of a rhizome can be connected to any other, and must be. This is very different from the tree or root, which plots a point, fixes an order" (7). The turns in teaching perspectives and practices we sought in the TEACH Project were toward attempting to cultivate classroom interactions and activities into a rhizome-like system that reached for and cultivated multiple entryways to learning with novel connectivities and the promotion of a democracy of ideas. We felt the mediational roles of teachers and the multimodal affordances of digital texts and tools were key to a rhizomatic shift.

This shift is aided because the core interactions between teachers and learners—including the relationships, roles, and rules they are realized through—can be fundamentally changed when learning is mediated with a remix of digital texts and tools. There are several conceptualizations for mediating learning that informed our project. For example, Feuerstein's work (Feuerstein et al. 2002, 2004) provided insights for considering the nature of new roles for teachers in mediating learning. His focus on the interaction between the learner and materials or tools for learning like books or computers acknowledged that direct learning can occur without assistance. But his models and theories powerfully revealed how direct learning can be significantly extended when a mediator intercedes between the learner and other learning materials or tools. The mediator guides learners to interact more productively by systematically modifying their interactions and responses to learning materials in order to continually increase the learners' levels of understanding. In the TEACH Project, we benefited from the general conceptual framing of mediation in Feuerstein's work, but we did not in any way attempt to employ his systematic Mediated Learning Experience model because we did not have the extensive training needed for this comprehensive approach.

Rather, the TEACH approach was to utilize the five CREDE standards for effective pedagogy that we trained V-Tech teachers in as foundational guides to what they would actually do while mediating student learning. These guides were augmented by our approach to project-based learning as well as by concepts from Chavez and Soep's (2005) collegial pedagogy. In enacting CREDE's first standard of joint productive activity, for example, teachers mediate student learning as experts engaging novices as they work toward joint products and learning goals. This form of mediation substantively consists of engaging students in planned, goal-directed dialogues called instructional conversations, as delineated in standard 5 that connect academic content to the students' prior knowledge and experiences as indicated in standard 3. Mediating learning through these kinds of classroom dialogues is a pivot point in the turn of teachers because it is through these conversations that the knowledge, skills, values, and culture of the learner are revealed, enabling the teacher to contextualize teaching to fit the learner's background, experiences, and interests. As noted earlier in this chapter and throughout this book, prior knowledge and experiences for many students are highly influenced by hip-hop culture. So, through instructional conversations, teachers make these connections in conjunction with their designs of challenging, complex projects and tasks for learning as reflected in standard 4. Augmenting this approach to mediation are processes to have the students themselves jointly frame projects and share in accountability for the work. These projects would frequently have an emphasis on social change as well as on students taking increasing leadership in inquiry learning as delineated by the collegial pedagogy of Chavez and Soep (2005). The combined elements of this systematic approach to mediating learning work to negate the deficit presuppositions of remediation approaches that have primarily been used with students like those at V-Tech by building on their diverse capabilities, interests, and strengths rather than focusing on weaknesses.

CREDE standards are based on Vygotsky's (1978) formulations of the social nature of learning—that learning occurs in the zone of proximal development (ZPD) through social interaction and discourse with teachers or peers acting as more knowledgeable others. This approach to mediating learning is not dependent on the use of digital technology, but other considerations attend when teachers remix digital texts and tools into learning activities. When this happens, mediation of learning also occurs through students engaging the material intelligence of digital devices. It acts as a "third participant" in the sociocultural process of learning and, at some level, is able to perform the role of "expert" (teacher) in the ZPD in guiding, differentiating, and creating appropriate levels of challenge for learners to progress from novices to experts. Examples of students learning through the material intelligence in digital tools are described in Ms. Foster and Ms. Young's classes, and further analysis of how this worked to guide their students' learning is provided in chapters 2, 4, and 5.

The concept of material intelligence is somewhat similar to but not as comprehensive as actor-network theory (ANT), an approach to social theory and research that originated in the field of science and technology studies. ANT offers a range of material-semiotic approaches and theories that locate agency in networks of associations between humans and nonhuman objects (Callon 1989; Latour 2005; Law and Hassard 1999). Beginning in the 1990s, ANT spread beyond the field of science and technology studies to become a popular tool for analysis of large-scale networks in a wide range of fields. However, the more limited focus of the concept of material intelligence regarding affordances of specific digital tools was more useful in the TEACH Project for seeing the ways that teachers needed to incorporate mediating capacities of the digital devices into their own mediational roles in the learning of their students.

Another feature we felt teachers needed to bring into the mediation of student learning was the collective intelligence that could be easily accessed with digital media. The power of collective intelligence in facilitating the generation, evaluation, and synthesis of ideas to increase student learning was demonstrated in the early PD sessions and realized in both the learning of teachers in professional development as described in chapter 3 and the learning of students as discussed in chapters 2, 4, and 5. In conjunction with and as a consequence of affordances of material and collective intelligence in new media, the teachers needed to not only accept but also reconceive how they enacted their mediational roles. This was especially apparent when considering possibilities for their students learning in multi-user virtual environments—how material, collective, and personal intelligence are "embodied" in digital spaces and how knowledge is gained and changed (linked and overlapped through multiple realities and identities) in virtual worlds.

In reconceiving mediational roles for these learning environments, the notion of "place" that is used in architecture and urban design was important. Learning in virtual environments is predicated on being able to establish a sense of place (a sense of rootedness in an understood reality). In other words, learning experiences are "situated" (they take place in a "place") in such a way as to be familiar to the learner. This notion of place is important in order for learners to feel both connectedness and distinctiveness in virtual environments. It is enabled by the material intelligence designed into digital media and the collective intelligence that the media facilitates. It requires learners to produce and probe for meanings in multimodal, semiotic domains of virtual worlds and to be more active, critical learners.

New National Educational Technology Standards and Performance Indicators for teachers (appendix A) and students (appendix B) that are being adopted in the United States and other countries are beginning to address the need for teachers to design, develop, and model digital-age learning, assessment, and work experiences for students. Developed as benchmarks by the International Society for Technology in Education (ISTE), these standards are increasingly being seen as central to the professional growth and leadership development of educators. This book shows how the work of V-Tech teachers connected to many of these new standards for technology in education. In the context of new demands and possibilities enabled by technology, the role of teachers in mediating student learning has become more critical rather than less so.

To effectively enact these critical roles, teachers, administrators, and staff at V-Tech worked to transform the culture and structure of their school to better engage, enrich, and enable their students to meet the challenges of life and learning in the twenty-first century. Clearly, through the TEACH Project, considerable resources were brought into the school to support the teachers' learning and work to enact new perspectives, so aspects of what was achieved might not be reproducible in some educational settings. Nevertheless, this work to ameliorate the learning of marginalized students contributes to understanding how to better design educational experiences for a far wider range of students. It starts with teachers like Ms. Glide and her colleagues who were able to make a fundamental turn in their teaching perspectives and practices. Initially technophobic, Ms. Glide learned to mediate her students' learning with a range of digital texts and tools and eventually led her students on learning expeditions in the virtual world of Teen Second Life. At the end of the school year, she reported, "I developed a genuine interest and excitement as I acquired new skills and have seen this manifest itself in my teaching practice. In turn, I have observed similar engagement from my students when technology is a part of their learning." Together, the V-Tech teachers mediated a vital remix of learning that cultivated new roots and shoots of rhizomatic growth and intellectual connectivity.

2 | HIP-HOP JOURNALISM

During the 2007–8 school year, students in Ms. Foster's Hip-Hop Journalism class learned to use a number of digital tools that directly connected to her curricular goals of developing their skills with traditional and new media literacies. They created digital photography projects and blogs, digital stories and PowerPoint presentations, youth commentaries and podcasts, and lyrics and digital beats. They also wrote texts related to these projects and completed other writing assignments. Essentially, these students were using technological resources to sample, cut and paste, and remix multimedia texts for replay in new configurations through "digital DJ-ing" that reflected aspects of contemporary hip-hop culture. In the process, they were learning to access, understand, critique, and produce a variety of texts—including written texts—through project-based activities that utilized the strategies and tools of journalists.

This focus on working with students to develop journalistic skills using digital media was central to Ms. Foster's instructional approach. It extended in part from discussions early on in the school's PD sessions about effective ways to transform classroom dynamics for teaching and learning. In one PD session, we discussed the provocative book *Our America* (1997) by Lloyd Newman and LeAlan Jones as an example of powerful ways that young people could learn about the world and contribute to the learning of others as journalists. I shared research I had published on an underperforming urban school a few miles from V-Tech where a teacher had developed a successful curriculum unit in which her students did research, writing, and portfolio projects modeled on considerations from the book (Mahiri and Conner 2003).

LeAlan and Lloyd were guided and supported in their work by radio producer David Isay. At 14, these two African American boys began documenting and writing about life and death in the Ida B. Wells Housing Project in Chicago. In addition to the book, their work was also presented as two National Public Radio "special reports" in the late 1990s.

The second NPR special, "Remorse: The Fourteen Stories of Eric Morse," won broadcasting's highest honor—the George Foster Peabody Award. In one of the many tributes to these young men in the front matter of the book, Adam Matthews of the *Source* wrote that they "convey a reality and an urgency from which even the most learned academics and so called experts fall short, and in the process usher in a new stylistic vanguard of sensitive, first-person, urban journalism."

During professional development, we talked about the viability of positioning students as journalists in each academic discipline, particularly in light of affordances of new media that have significantly increased the techniques and tools for accessing and producing information. This comes at a time when our understanding of what constitutes journalism is being challenged and changed. This was dramatically exemplified in the case of video blogger Josh Wolf. By refusing to testify or turn over his videotape of a protest against a G8 summit, he was sent to federal prison for 226 days. His case fueled debates about who is entitled to protections of the press like the right to maintain the confidentiality of sources (Berton 2008). In essence, it is a debate about who can claim to be a journalist as technology enables new ways to write and rewrite societal narratives.

In addition to the emphasis of our PD sessions, Ms. Foster's appreciation of pedagogical possibilities based on a journalism perspective was also linked to her work with Youth Radio. Before being hired at V-Tech, she developed curriculum materials for teachers based on the digital productions of youth in this community-based organization. It has trained thousands of teenagers in broadcast journalism, production, engineering, and media advocacy since 1992. "At V-Tech," Ms. Foster noted, "I wanted to see if we could engage students like they do at Youth Radio." Supporting and observing her teaching helped us address central questions of the TEACH Project like what key possibilities and problems were associated with significant uses of digital media for teaching and learning in the school and what implications this approach had for wider school settings.

Ms. Foster was comfortable with me sitting in on her class, and over the school year, I observed and took field notes more than 40 times. Her only request was that I periodically let her read the field notes I wrote on my laptop during each visit. I was happy to comply. The class met during the first block of instruction every day except Fridays. The principal had structured the first period of school as a two-hour block for several elective class offerings, to support the students' overall academic development with engaging topics and also to help motivate them to get to school on time. As noted earlier, consistent attendance was a continual problem at the school. In her class, Ms. Foster had 24 students who pretty much reflected the demographics of the school: 7 black women, 5 Latina women, 10 black men, and 2 Latino men. I did formal interviews with Ms. Foster at the beginning, middle, and end of the school year and had many informal conversations with her and others who provided instructional and other support to this class. She also provided written narratives and reflections on her teaching as well as teacher-initiated surveys of student perspectives on different aspects of activities in the class. Additionally, two members of the TEACH research team did observations in the class and wrote descriptive and analysis notes. Importantly, the digital media itself conserved the products of the students' work for subsequent assessment and review.

Ms. Foster is an African American teacher who holds a master's degree in education as well as credentials in Spanish and French. She was 32 years old at the beginning of the 2007–8 school year, when she was hired to teach Spanish at the school. Clearly, she was already inclined to teach through a more task-oriented, hands-on approach rather than a more lecture-oriented style. Because she was a veteran teacher with seven years of experience—more than most of the other teachers—the principal and I "informally" asked her to take the lead in piloting the use of digital media in conjunction with the TEACH focus on professional development. She selected to do this primarily in the elective course Hip-Hop Journalism. She came up with the course's title to signal a curricular focus on topics that were relevant and of interest to young people, including issues surrounding youth culture, global events, social class, gender, and race. She later found that the students' use of digital media to engage these issues also reflected aspects of hip-hop culture. At the beginning of the first semester, the principal stopped by and talked with Ms. Foster about her plans for the class. Again, he affirmed his desire and support for the class to provide examples of the viability of digitally mediated learning. "I would like for this to be a model class," he said. "Set up some technology stations. This could be a place to show what we want other teachers to do. Be on me to get things outta here that are not needed. I'm big on aesthetics."

THE WORLD WIDE WALL

Midway through the academic year, 10 Mac iBook laptops that were carted to the classroom on a mobile computer lab were stolen in a break-in that occurred after school. After this event, the principal turned one classroom into a dedicated computer lab that had 12 desktop computers, 5 of which were new iMacs. However, the students in Ms. Foster's class lost a lot of their work that had been saved on the laptops but not backed up elsewhere. Consequently, she had all of her students get Gmail (Google) accounts so that the things they produced could be saved, accessed, and modified online at school and at home. She noticed that many of her students created their Gmail accounts with "RIP" (rest in peace) and the name of someone close to them who had died. She saw this form of memorializing as part of their attempts to deal with the tragic losses of loved ones that so many of her students had experienced.

An African American male in her class who I will call DeShawn (pseudonyms are used for everyone named) was one such student. A close friend of his had just been killed in gang-related violence. For a class assignment, he wrote an essay about his friend's life and death. After class that day, Ms. Foster found DeShawn's username tagged in big letters on a table. The next day, she asked him to clean it off, and he did. A few days later, Ms. Foster had her class go to the computer lab and sign up for blogs. Like most of the students, DeShawn was excited about creating his own web page, and he stayed in the lab after the class ended to work on his blog while listening to music on the computer. A counselor who came into the lab and did not know what DeShawn was working on told him to turn off the music and go to his next class. DeShawn reacted to the tone of the counselor's request, and an intense verbal exchange ensued that resulted in him being suspended for a couple of days.

Upon returning to school, DeShawn was still determined to create his blog, motivated by his desire to pay tribute to his friend. He uploaded his essay and then went to work uploading pictures of his friend to an online photo album that he wanted to post as a slideshow with a musical background on his blog. But neither Ms. Foster nor other students in the class knew how to create a slideshow in a blog. So DeShawn struggled and experimented on his own until he discovered how to run the slideshow on his blog site. His excitement at the moment of this accomplishment was apparent to everyone in the class, and he invited others to come over and see what he had done. He described his blog as a "world wide wall." It had allowed him to make a specific cultural practice accessible globally. In the process, he helped make it officially "cool" to have a blog in the class. His enthusiasm was contagious, even spreading to another class. For example, when his social studies teacher also did a blog project, DeShawn brought what he had learned in his journalism class to the task. He became the resident "expert" in the social studies class on technical aspects of creating blogs, providing guidance and assistance to other classmates. "Y'all makin' me feel weird," he told Ms. Foster at one point as she praised his success with this project. "I ain't never got so much positive attention up at the schoolhouse."

This story of the World Wide Web being appropriated as a "world wide wall" reflected a number of ways that teaching and learning were changing in Ms. Foster's class. She had established an active learning context in which DeShawn and his classmates moved back and forth between traditional and new media literacies while connecting to their unique experiences and interests. In so doing, they engaged new principles of learning that facilitated individual leadership and peer-to-peer collaborations on meaning making and problem solving. In this chapter, I further describe how these changes were enacted through project-based activities that utilized specific prompts to initiate learning processes that resulted in an array of products and presentations as well as written and other reflections. I explore how these changes reflected new principles of learning enabled by digital media, with its multimodalities, its semiotic domains, and its material intelligence and collective intelligence that combine to facilitate active, critical learning and probing to make meaning. I discuss how these changes reflected mediation through CREDE principles for effective instruction of joint productive activity; literacy development across disciplines; connecting academic content to students' prior knowledge and experiences; instructional conversations; and engaging students in challenging, complex tasks for learning. Elements of Youth Radio's collegial pedagogy overlap with some of CREDE's principles, but I additionally show how youth-led inquiry was encouraged, how accountability was distributed among participants, and how student work was connected to attempts at influencing social change beyond school.

YOUNG JOURNALISTS

Since it was important to Ms. Foster and the TEACH Project to incorporate perspectives from Youth Radio, the principal provided funds for a person from that organization to work with the journalism class during the first semester of the academic year. Ms. Foster recruited Ms. Young, a 19-year-old Youth Radio intern who had been working for about a year as a photographer, youth commentator, and online producer. While consulting for Youth Radio, Ms. Foster had developed curriculum ideas for teachers that were posted on the organization's website. Several of these were based on radio commentaries that had been produced and aired by this young journalist.

Only a year or two older than students in the class, Ms. Young was an African American woman who connected to them in more ways than just her youth or race. She grew up in a nearby city known locally and nationally for its high rates of poverty, violence, and crime. In her work at Youth Radio, she has produced more than 35 commentaries, photo essays, and other projects for the organization's website and radio programs, and several of her works had been aired on National Public Radio. Her topics ranged from political events to art openings, but a number of them also focused on violence and crime. For example, she wrote and produced commentaries comparing the shootings at a major university to the shootings in her neighborhood ("We get shot here every month") and comparing working for a corporation to prostitution in the hood ("Sellin' your soul"). In one of her commentaries, she told radio listeners,

> Shootings happen all the time in my city—I've even grown to expect them. But soon after my nineteenth birthday, there was one shooting that shook that attitude. It was my 17-year-old cousin Junior—my best friend. That night, I called around trying to get in touch with him. Junior's friend J-Rock said, "Oh, you ain't heard?" Right then, man, my heart dropped. He told me my cousin was shot.

Beyond this trauma (Ms. Young later found out that her cousin would be OK), Ms. Young's work clearly shows the journalism perspectives and skills that Ms. Foster wanted each of her students to develop. Ms. Young also possessed a framework for learning these things that had been shaped, in part, by her experiences as a Youth Radio intern. When I interviewed her about her ideas for collaborating with Ms. Foster at V-Tech, she said,

I think it's very important to have opportunities for leadership in this new school. Like here at Youth Radio, we youngsters take on the role of peer educators. A lot of us already have a lot of raw talent that needs a little polishing. With training we're able to deliver that knowledge to our friends while learning in the most effective manner. And the other thing I want to mention, we're put in real life situations and faced with real audiences here at Youth Radio. Use me for an example. I help a team of web designers build Youth Radio's brand-new website. I get to show off my work online and in a portfolio giving me opportunities to find additional work.

In Hip-Hop Journalism, Ms. Young worked with Ms. Foster to realize these ideas, along with other perspectives and skills promoted by TEACH that were observed at various levels in the digital projects, new principles of learning, and changing practices of teaching in the class.

DIGITAL PROJECTS

"On the first day of class," reflected Ms. Foster, "Ms. Young and I set a precedent. We never assigned our students any assignments that we were not willing to do ourselves." They were attempting to establish a culture of joint activities and joint accountability from the very start. "We also kept our class relevant to current events and personal experiences," she continued. "Sometimes we pushed students out of their comfort zones, but we always participated as well. We wrote poetry together, rapped together, put questions in balloons and popped them and then answered them, wrote headlines that reflected our lives ten years from now, and played musical chairs and other games." Ms. Foster felt that the foundation for learning was tied to building healthy, trusting relationships among all class participants—adults and students alike. Consequently, she started each class with a warm-up activity (what the National Urban Alliance for Effective Education calls "community builders") that she and Ms. Young scoured from educational websites and acting books.

Another core strategy revealed in Ms. Foster's teaching was to create projects and activities linked to contemporary events in ways that encouraged youth-led inquiries into societal issues and actions for social change. For example, during the first month of the new semester, she and Ms. Young accompanied students who had decided to go to a Jena

Six protest on a university campus close to V-Tech. On the same day, a young black man from the surrounding community who a number of V-Tech students knew was shot and killed by the police in what was later found to be a case of mistaken identity. Ms. Foster quickly developed a unit on stereotypes. She accessed Youth Radio's website in class to play and discuss one of Ms. Young's commentaries on violence in her hometown that originally aired on NPR. She also played and discussed a short video she had made about an incident in which she and two black men were racially profiled by police officers. She felt that using these digitally mediated personal narratives made discussions of critical social issues and events more viable. They certainly did not need to be made more real for her students because immediate experiences with intense social conditions were pervasive in many of their lives. But Ms. Foster felt that the different examples of presenting these issues with digital media allowed students to appreciate new possibilities for telling their own stories about social conditions that affected their lives.

Initial projects in the class mainly used digital photography, one of Ms. Young's major interests and strengths, with students learning how to edit and compose their work in Photoshop. Some of these projects culminated as photo essays and PowerPoint slideshows. Later in the semester, students worked a bit with video projects, but it was a while before the school had been able to install Final Cut Pro on several of the computers. As the year progressed, students created and communicated with blogs and used these sites to display their completed photography as well as some of their writing. Additionally, they learned to make music and beats using GarageBand, but this tool was mainly used for their youth commentary projects that were produced as podcasts.

I will discuss the development of a number of these digital projects, but first I want to provide a bit more insight into the dynamics of day-to-day activities in the class. Thus far, I have not fully illuminated the complexities of teaching and learning in this classroom (and school) context that surrounded development of the various digital projects. So, before looking at additional representative projects, I provide a portrait of the classroom dynamics—the patterns of interaction that emerged early in the school year—drawn from my field notes of a single but illustrative day in the first semester of the class (September 17, 2007). It is a depiction of what the teachers and students actually do and say while working in class, more so than what they say they do.

A Day in Class

The classroom is one of the nine "portables" that face each other—four on one side, five on the other—along the narrow grassy yard that runs down the center of the school's small campus. When the bell rings to start first period, there are seven students scattered around the large circle of chairs that take up half the space in the room. Of these seven students, three are new and have not been in previous classes. Two of these new students are twin Latina girls who immediately took seats next to two other Latinas. One Latina, Rosa, is present and on time for every class. She does all of the work but rarely says a word. Emma is the other Latina already in the class, and she also attends consistently. As they wait for class to start, Emma is sharing a song on her cell phone with one of the twins; each has one of the stereo earplugs in one ear.

All the other girls enrolled in the class are black. Two are present and talking quietly to each other. One of them, with her hair styled in corn-rows and dyed blond, is also new to the class. She refers to the other girl, Imani, with the "N" word, but it seems to be a normal part of their conversation, not adversarial. The same thing can be said for other curse words that flow in their streams of conversation. The other student present is Jamal, an African American male. He's sitting alone with head-phones on, bopping to the beat and audibly rapping along with a song: "To make hoes fit the track, and come back phat." Ms. Foster walks over and asks him to take the headphones off. As he complies, he says, "I got speakers in my ears, and I got speakers in my shoes." She doesn't respond to his comment and instead turns to greet a few more students who are trickling in.

"I'm sorry I'm late," Deja says as she goes to a seat. Maurice, Dar-nell, and Tyrone are right behind her, and they, too, find seats around the circle. These three African American males all have dreadlocks, and one has his dyed reddish brown. Like most of the students in the class, they are dressed similarly. All of the girls wear stylish, fitted jeans, while almost every boy has baggy jeans, a hooded sweatshirt, and unlaced bas-ketball shoes. Yet each one of these young men looks distinct, with dif-ferent kinds of sweatshirts in various colors and different styles of baggy jeans. Also, they all are wearing ball caps, which are often kept on during class. After about five more minutes, Jalen comes in. He always has lots of things to say about any topic being discussed in class. He is also notable because he doesn't wear baggy jeans and sweatshirts. Instead, his slacks or jeans are more fitted, and today he has on a black sport coat, a bright red silky shirt, and shiny black leather shoes. "I'm so tired. I shouldn't even be here," he announces to no one in particular. "I didn't get to sleep until three this morning."

Now there are 12 students present, approximately 15 minutes after the bell rang to start first period. Ms. Foster gets everyone's attention with an announcement of her plans to take the class on a field trip to Youth Radio. Next, she describes the day's community builder: "Write a headline that would lead off an article in a newspaper about how you want to be in the future. In other words if there was an article written about you in the future, what would people read about?" One male student refuses to participate and puts his head down on the desk. The others write headlines on scraps of paper and put them in a box. Then they each select a headline from the box, talk briefly about it, and try to guess who wrote it. Ms. Foster and Ms. Young write headlines, too. As the headlines are read, it's clear that some have been written seriously—"All the seniors at V-Tech have graduated on time"—and some have been written as jokes. Yet it works as a community builder in that students and teachers are talking to each other about their lives and their hopes for the future. Two more students, Aliyah and Andre, come in as the community builder comes to an end. The total number that attends class on this day is 14.

Ms. Foster next begins a more formal part of the class where she is having the students respond to two newspaper articles about the Jena Six by finding the main points and comparing the perspectives of the authors. She reads the first article and guides them in discussion and analysis of its key points. Then they read the second article and write an introductory paragraph for an essay that will assess the differing treatments of this provocative issue. They are asked to complete the essay for homework. With this work, Ms. Foster is attempting to build their capacities to critique the media both orally and in writing. Student interest is high because of the article's topic, but the student who would not participate earlier still keeps his head on the desk. While the discussion is going on, a cell phone rings. Darnell says, "My bad," and stops the ringing before Ms. Foster can say anything, although she does give him a look. It turns out that it's a text message saying, "What are you doing?" We learn this because, to Ms. Foster's and everyone else's amazement, Darnell reads the message out loud. Then he answers it out loud to the now captive audience of the class. "I'm in school. What you think I'm doin'?" he says, as if the texter was in the room. "This is like when you get a call at five in the morning asking what you doin'. I'm sleep. What you think I'm doin'?" Ms. Foster tells him they need to meet during the break.

As the activity on the articles comes to an end, Ms. Young sets up her computer and LCD projector in the middle of the circle and focuses it on a large screen on one of the room's sidewalls. She uses this format to both tell and show students what she is doing on her computer and what she wants them to do on theirs. While Ms. Young is setting up, Ms. Foster is issuing laptop computers to the students from the mobile computer cart. The one young man who was not engaged earlier noticeably perks up when the computers come out. There are 10 laptops from the cart and five desktops lined up on the far wall of the classroom. So everyone is able to work individually on a computer, but most choose to work in pairs. Also, the laptops are preferred over the desktops.

Today, Ms. Young has the students going online to get images in order to work with them further in Photoshop. The specific task is for students to learn how to merge and edit two images by first finding a website that has a large-screen TV and then using Photoshop to merge that image with a photo uploaded from a digital camera, editing the final image so that the photo appears to be on the TV's screen. The photos in the camera were taken in a previous class, and most of them were of the students themselves. So the final effect was having images of students in the class appearing to be on TV. "When you get to Photoshop, what is the first thing you do?" Ms. Young asks. Students shout out a variety of answers. "There's nothing you can do until you unlock the background," she continues. "Once it's in iPhoto, it's locked in there." She asks Deja to come up and go through the process of uploading photos from one of the digital cameras. Deja takes over operating the computer, and Ms. Young guides her through uploading the pictures.

At one point, the computer freezes, and students start offering suggestions for how to unfreeze it. Andre says, "What you do is close down the program and get out of Photoshop, and then start the program over again." This gets the computer working again.

Ms. Young commissions Andre, who is already skilled with Photoshop, to help her and Ms. Foster go around and work individually with the new students and any others who have problems working on the assignment. Someone asks what the word *megapixels* means, and Ms.

Young explains, "The more megapixels you have, the sharper the picture comes out." There is continual chatter around the classroom as students work together and help each other out. They are able to figure out a lot of the technical details of what they are doing. Most students seem to be on task. A couple try to go on to Myspace, but the school blocks it. Jamal is reciting raps while working, but he is clearly doing the project.

As work continues, a school staff member comes by and leaves a large basket of food—milk, dry cereal, juice, muffins, yogurt, and an assortment of fruit—on a table by the entrance. Soon, Ms. Foster gives the students their 15-minute break. During the break, students select snacks and go outside to mingle with friends from other elective classes who are also on break. Ms. Foster's desk is in the far corner of one side of the room with the entrance at the other corner. Her desk is pretty big, so the corner is like a separate module in the larger classroom. She and Darnell have a quick conversation there, and he apologizes about the cell phone incident. He also agrees to apologize to the class. As he goes out, Aliyah comes over and talks to Ms. Foster about plans to get a job at an amusement park 35 miles away. Ms. Foster is concerned about the commute, and Aliyah tells her that it's only on the weekends. She also tells her that she is currently staying with a friend, "until my mom gets her stuff together." Outside, Imani shows Ms. Young some moves she has learned from a girls' dance group that recently formed at the school. Ms. Young is in a dance class at the community college she attends, and she reciprocates by showing Imani some steps too. She has just started wearing her hair in braids, and Imani comments, "I see you got twisted up; it looks nice." All during the break, Deja continues to work on the photo assignment, and I ask her why. She answers, "I just wanted to understand how to work with Photoshop, to mess with things, see what they're like."

After the break, Ms. Young begins by projecting more pictures that the students have previously taken with the digital cameras onto the big screen. A student who doesn't belong in the class came in with the others returning from break. He sat at a vacant computer station, intensely observing what was going on. When Ms. Foster notices him, she comes over and ushers him to the door. Meanwhile, Ms. Young is showing one of the pictures that a student took of a tattoo on his arm to demonstrate the importance of having a neutral background when editing a photo: "When you have a white background, it's easier to manipulate the picture. So while working in Photoshop, you need to give the main image a solid background." She models additional editing techniques with the pictures they have taken of themselves: "Another thing I was telling you guys is that when you see something doesn't fit, you can 'blur' to make things fit." The students are smiling and commenting, and their attention is keenly focused on the screen (although Emma has slipped an earplug for her iPod into one ear).

A short time after the students have gone back to their individual work, the school's security officer comes in and makes a short announcement: "We all know that there is a funeral today, and some of you guys have decided to go. We have to let you know that if you go and you don't get back for your third-period class, your parents will be called. And, at the last few funerals [he names the city where Ms. Young lives], there have been drive-bys at the funeral. So please be careful." I'm surprised that the students don't really diverge from their work to talk about this. There are a few side conversations, but, mainly, they continue to work toward completion of the day's classwork. Shortly before class ends, the principal comes in. Deja is sitting near the entrance, and she puts out her fist to bump fists with him. He does not initially see her, and she says, "Oh, you goin' to leave me hanging?" He turns to her, and they bump fists. He observes for about five minutes and then starts to leave. "What's up?" Maurice asks while calling the principal by his first name. "When we gonna start that revolution?" The principal replies, "It started two hours ago when you all got to class."

A number of considerations for teaching and learning are depicted in this class portrait, which is presented here in order to frame the following descriptions of work on digital projects throughout the academic year. These projects began with digital photography and continued with PowerPoint presentations and digital stories, blogs, and the production of youth commentaries and podcasts. These are important tools for accessing and creating meaning and for making social impacts and connections. In the following discussions, I will show more of how these students learned to use these tools for academic development as well as to amplify their voices and views on critical issues that affected their lives.

The Magazine Project

At the beginning of the school year, technology resources for the journalism class were sparse. There was the mobile computer lab, but the laptops had very little software on them to facilitate the teachers' ambitious plans for the class. The class also did not have digital cameras and photo printers or voice recorders initially. Students joked about how going to V-Tech with no technology was like going to a Chinese restaurant where there's no rice or a KFC where there's no chicken. The principal had ordered a number of needed items, but the administrative structure of the school district was painfully slow. To facilitate activities for the first month of classes, I used TEACH resources in order to purchase several digital cameras, a photo printer, a desktop computer, and higher-end speakers. When the cameras and printer were delivered to the class, Ms. Foster started poring over the instruction booklets. In comparison, Emma and Deja immediately started unpacking and setting up the new equipment—putting in the memory cards and batteries, connecting them with the appropriate cables and power cords, and setting the time and date functions. Jalen commented while observing this scene, "I feel like I'm in one of those movies like *Freedom Writers* or something, where kids don't have anything."

There were numerous examples of students like DeShawn staying after class or Deja working through the break to continue with their projects. Deja's work in Photoshop was a good example of ways this project was stimulating student learning. The initial work in Photoshop evolved into a project of the students creating an article for a magazine with appropriate graphics to support their written texts. "We need some ideas to write about," one student yelled out after hearing that writing was a key part of the project. They got some of their ideas from assignments to read and critique selected magazine articles. Some students were surprised to see that even the hip-hop magazines like *Vibe* and the *Source* were written in language styles more reflective of the academy than the streets. Similarly, they found that the blogs of several local hip-hop journalists, like Davey D, were written in Standard English. The final goal was to combine all of the articles, add a cover and table of contents, and eventually print it in paper copies.

In setting up the project, Ms. Young announced, "I'm about to show you guys an example of a magazine cover that I did last night in Photoshop. I did everything in layers. I took this picture in [a nearby city]." She projected a beautifully done mock cover of an African American woman with a city scene in the background. "I took this picture from up on the thumbnails and dragged it to Photoshop," she continued, and then she gave the following step-by-step demonstration of how she had worked on parts of the example magazine cover.

The magic wand I used to select a big body of color for the background. If I need to delete something, what I do is go over and click on the magic wand. If it was a whole lot of stuff in the background, I would not be able to erase the background that easily. This thing right here is used to drag everything around. But it's locked, so I have to click on it. If I want to, I can make the background another color; I can make the background another photo. When you work in Photoshop, you want to do everything in layers so that when you mess up you don't have to start all over again.

When she finished the demonstration, she let the students practice in Photoshop and work on their magazine assignment, telling them, "Go online and get a picture, and start making your graphics." In her approach to demonstrating how to work with the media, she also modeled and provided opportunities for the students to work in similar ways on their own and with peers as well as with adults.

I observed Deja for a while as she worked on her magazine project. Earlier, she had been writing fluidly to compose her text. Then she shifted to working on the images. As she worked, she talked to me about what she had done so far.

I went to Google and got this 500 × 500 megapixel picture, and dragged it to the Photoshop icon. When you click on that, it automatically gives you a perfect size of the picture you choose. You can get a picture from anywhere and it will also be able to be dragged to the Photoshop icon. Then you click and merge the layers so you take one picture and drag it on top of the other picture.

I went to the first layer and erased the background of it so that my picture would show up. You can go to filter gallery, and it has different kinds of textures you can use for your photo. Then you have to adjust your picture with the picture gallery. I went to filter gallery. They give you different types of textures, and I clicked on the one that looked like a crayonlike texture, and it put that onto my original picture.

There was a clear correspondence between how Deja was able to describe what she had done and Ms. Young's explicit directions for what the students should do. Deja's growing expertise in using Photoshop excited her, and she worked intensely on both composing the written text and creating the graphics for her article. "It's a new way of learning," she told me. "It's faster and more fun." As it turns out, the class never actually produced the paper version of the magazine. But when I asked Deja later how she felt about the magazine project, she said, "Hey, we went stupid on our pictures. I loved doing it. We went stupid."[1]

Almost every student shared Deja's enthusiasm for the projects they were doing in the class. A few students, like Malik and Andre, were even more skilled than Deja because they had prior experiences working with digital media for their own purposes outside of school. For example, Malik was a student who joined the class after the magazine project was well under way, but he quickly caught up with everyone else. When he entered class for the first time, another student immediately said, "Oh, we got a new student in the class. Introduce yourself." The students stopped what they were doing and listened as he told them his name and a couple things he likes to do. He said he liked to rap (he has a "gold grill" on his teeth) and that he was really into sports. When the class started working on an assignment, he went over to the computer, got online, and showed Ms. Foster his Photobucket website. He had numerous photos posted, and Ms. Foster commented about how they were nicely done. It was clear that he already had some of the skills that were being taught to the students. Ms. Foster told him that it would be great if he could help other students. But Malik said, "I'm not good at explaining stuff; I just know how to do it." She suggested that he think about checking out Youth Radio in order to further develop his interests and talents.

Digital Stories

Ms. Young led the work on the photography projects, but Ms. Foster designed and guided the work on all of the other digital projects in the class. The idea was to jump-start the class by immediately working with digital media while Ms. Foster was getting new ideas and gaining confidence in using digital tools in the PD sessions. As the semester progressed, she became more and more comfortable with trying in class the things she was learning in professional development. She worked extensively to have her students create blogs (exemplified earlier), digital stories rendered in PowerPoint, and youth commentaries that were eventually produced as podcasts. She also had her students work a bit with writing lyrics and making digital beats that were sometimes integrated into their other projects, and she developed activity centers in different areas of the classroom to support the kind of work being done on the specific projects.

PowerPoint presentations have become common in some schools, but most of the students in Ms. Foster's class had never actually created and delivered one before. This was particularly true for Rosa, who was always present, very soft-spoken, and extremely shy. She rarely talked in class, except to her friends. I initially thought she was not engaged, but I found, instead, that she had a different style of participation. In one of her essays, she described herself as "always listening, always quiet, always thinking about others." As I noted earlier, she did all of her assignments in the class, and I came to see that she was tuned in to everything that happened, but she was more comfortable being quiet and actively listening. She was challenged by a digital story project because one of the requirements after writing and rendering the story in a PowerPoint format was to present it to the class. Her story was about an incident her family had experienced, involving racial profiling by the police in her neighborhood. She told Ms. Foster that she could not present her story in front of the class. However, after she completed her PowerPoint that combined written text, images, and music, she realized that the story kind of told itself. The class watched and listened intently to her digital story, and it prompted lots of questions. Rosa was able to respond to their questions and provide more background and details about her story. Afterward, her classmates made comments like "That is the most I've ever heard her talk." Later, when Ms. Foster asked her how she was able to do it, she replied, "No one was looking at me." She felt they were focused on the images, words, and sounds in the digital medium she had produced rather than on her personally.

Podcasts

Like the digital stories, Ms. Foster also used youth commentary projects to develop and amplify her students' voices as hip-hop journalists. In the second semester of the school year, she had her students do a number of these projects linked to their ongoing critiques of traditional media as well as the productions of their own media. These projects would begin with writing prompts on current issues and events and how they were portrayed in contemporary media. Then some of the students' written work would be turned into youth commentaries ultimately produced as podcasts. Ms. Foster provided models for her students' projects from the Youth Radio website. Produced by young people like her students, the Youth Radio reporting styles in commentaries and "news breaks" were engaging, and the content was timely and relevant. Since the audio broadcasts were accompanied by written transcripts on the website, these models were particularly useful for struggling readers and writers.

With this curricular focus, Ms. Foster guided students in generating ideas to spark an inquiry process that utilized web-based resources to get information that they collaboratively subjected to analysis in order to develop critical perspectives. During the work on these projects, Ms. Foster would engage individuals and small groups of students in mediated interventions to help them broaden and complicate their understanding of the issues. She would elicit their experiential knowledge but expand it with information from textual and digital sources. Interestingly, she came to see that the use of digital sources actually facilitated deep explorations of controversial or emotional issues like race and racism, gender, oppression, incarceration, and violence. Students revised and refined their writing, and they learned how to transform their perspectives into journalistic commentaries and produced some of them as podcasts.

I will conclude this part of the chapter by discussing the podcast projects in terms of key issues that were addressed by students in the Hip-Hop Journalism class. Most were communicated in the style of short, verbal essays, while some were spoken word pieces. The process for producing these podcasts began with individual and collaborative research on issues, using online sources as well as articles and books. The students also wrote and edited a number of drafts of the texts to be podcasted. They worked in teams when using the GarageBand program on the Mac computers to digitally record, merge, and edit the audio tracks and other sound effects. Their commentaries focused on a wide range of issues, but there were three major, recurring themes. One consistent theme dealt with getting an education and achieving goals in life. Another major theme dealt with problems of youth, like pregnancies, injuries, drugs, violence, incarceration, and health. A final provocative theme dealt with experiences and critiques of race and racism in society. I will provide examples from three podcasts that reflect each of these themes to give a sense of the substance of the students' work, even though I have excerpted considerably from the complete audio texts.

One of Aliyah's podcasts was framed as a letter to young people but was addressed specifically to a female cousin, to have her rethink her life choices and goals.

> Have you ever thought about going to college? If you haven't, at least think about it. It doesn't have to be the top college in the world, but that would be nice. You can go to a community college or a two-year college

to get your associate's degree. But that's just like getting your high school diploma. Do you know what you want to be after you graduate? You might want to start thinking about that because time is going to pass faster than you think. I still don't know what I want to do. But, I can do hair, so that's a little kick push for me. . . . I would like to stay in school because it's something I want to do. . . . My mom and my dad didn't go to college and they're always working these mediocre jobs and always struggling. I would like to go to college, and me being the youngest, I think it's best for me.

Jalen's podcast on post-traumatic stress syndrome was a riveting comparison of the mental health conditions of some soldiers returning from war and the experiences that conditioned his mental and physical health growing up with violence.

PTSS stands for post-traumatic stress syndrome. This term is usually used for veterans of war. It would usually occur when soldiers would see someone shot, when they were shell shocked, or any traumatic event that would happen in the line of fire. Because this disorder does not necessarily cause any bleeding or the soldier does not lose a limb, it is not considered a wound, and the soldier does not get a purple heart for having it. . . . It is passed off as just a condition that therapy can cure or stabilize. . . . I personally have had PTSS for a little more than 12 years. Of course, not through war because I am only 18, but through my life's challenging events and the mental pictures stuck in my head. For example, seeing my sister beat up men and women because they owed her money. . . . Seeing my cousin shoot three boys who happened to be no older than me at the time. Or, even when I seen my older brother sell crack to his aunt. . . . Like soldiers, I have had therapy and anger management . . . for ten years. . . . [But] these sessions have failed. I currently suffer from anxiety attacks and what doctors say is a cycle of migraines. I take medicine for both of these conditions.

Tyrone's podcast on racial inequities was in spoken word style, and it ended with the line "Racism equals prejudice plus power," which also would be a good title for the piece.

I look in the mirror, double take on my face.
Running cold water on my scalp
I question the true meaning of race.
Africans were captured from Africa with no trace.
Slavery trapped human beings, no chance to escape.
And it still goes on today.
My question is, why and what for?

I stress the message with emphasis.
What is institutional oppression?
What about white supremacy?
No answers Mr. Governor? What is you givin' me?
Tell me why it's a sin to be young, black, male?
So much negative energy
Directing me straight to the jail cell. . . .
And I can't talk about this in a song
Because I'm afraid it won't sell . . .

In February of 2008, Ms. Foster's students participated in a conference at a nearby university and conducted a workshop in which they presented their podcasts and blog commentaries to faculty members and graduate students there. Her students also filed and disseminated their commentaries digitally and put a collection of them on a CD to share with friends, families, and fellow students. Some introduced their commentaries by saying things like "Hi, this is Jalen. I'm a hip-hop journalist." Seeing their work as an extension of hip-hop culture was important to them. Kitwana (2002) contends that more than anything else, hip-hop has helped to shape contemporary black youth culture as well as youth cultural production globally. Like the authors of *Our America*, these students came to take their work as young journalists very seriously. Adam Matthews's characterization of Lloyd and LeAlan's book applies, in some measure, to the work these V-Tech students produced, in that the students' work also conveys "a reality and an urgency . . . [through] a new stylistic vanguard of sensitive, first-person, urban journalism." In talking about her class, Ms. Foster noted, "It's the human aspect that strikes me the most in reading all the digital texts . . . [overcoming] a fear of public speaking, mourning the loss of your friend, empowering one's self with the knowledge to transcend." With each digital project, students were able to build on their experiences and interests to increase their learning, expand their critical analysis skills, and develop important new skills with digital media.

NEW LEARNING PRINCIPLES

Surveys of the students' perceptions about the use of computers in the journalism class revealed that they felt greatly facilitated and even inspired to do research as an engaging way to learn. As one student reported in our anonymous survey about using computers in the class, "You can look up info, voice your opinion, listen to music, watch videos, et cetera." Another student wrote, "It gives me other options for work." An additional student noted, "It's easy to get information off of computers, so that's the first source I turn to instead of books." One student claimed, "Whenever I have to research stuff for class, I start learning better." These perceptions were strongly affirmed by a student who wrote, "Technology expands my mind each day as I research every day what I need to learn." There were also a few drawbacks mentioned: "Sometimes they move slow"; "Some sites are blocked"; "I hate typing." But another student replied, "It has made writing easier." Based on their experiences with computer-based learning in the class, the students were also asked what they would like to learn more about. Examples of their responses were "the history behind computers," "the engineering of them," "sound and graphic design," and "how to use a computer good." Another ambitious response was "I would like to know how to build a computer and about how to really make my own website like the blogger. I like that a lot."

The students' understanding of the importance of doing research as a key way to learn was directly linked to their use of computers, the Internet, and other digital media for their work on various projects during the school year. In this section, I discuss how the digital photography, digital storytelling, blogs, and podcast projects they did reflected new principles of learning. Of the 36 learning principles defined by Gee (2004), the TEACH Project focused on 6 that we found to be useful for framing the work with digital media at the school: the multimodal principle (how meaning and knowledge are built up through various modalities, not just words); the semiotic principle (that learning involves interrelations with and across multiple, complex sign systems that form semiotic domains); the material intelligence principle (that thinking, problem solving, and knowledge are already stored in material objects); the probing principle (that learning is a cycle of probing and continually reflecting in and on this action); and the active, critical learning principle (that the environment created by new principles of learning encourages learning to be active and critical, rather than passive); and the "distributive principle" (that meaning and knowledge are distributed across the learner, objects, tools, symbols, technologies, and the environment). Ultimately, as Shaffer (2006) argued, rather than focusing on the digital media itself, what is important are these new ways of thinking and learning that it enables.

Words, still images, moving images, and sounds are significantly more accessible and able to be manipulated in constructions and remixes of meaning using digital media. The writing in this book, by comparison, mainly communicates in just one of these mediums. So, although I tried to represent the work on digital projects in the class through writing, much is lost by not being able to elicit more of the vibrancy of these multimodal collages of visual, audible, and tactile sign systems. A basic cell phone's capabilities to provide voice, music, pictures, video, a variety of written texts, Internet access, and much more exemplifies affordances of digital devices to integrate and allow one to manipulate multiple expressive modes. As Horst and Miller (2006) showed in their study of cell phone use in Jamaica, the social consequences can be both dramatic and unanticipated as varying potentialities of the technology are appropriated for different contexts and purposes. This was also the case in the journalism class, where both planned and unanticipated uses of digital technology influenced the learning and social dynamics of the class in novel ways.

In addressing new principles of learning revealed in the work on student projects, I will also reference a few instances of unanticipated uses of cell phones in the class. In the earlier description of class activities, for example, Emma shared music on her phone with one of the twins before class formally started (each with one of the stereo earplugs in one ear). In so doing, she seemed to be welcoming the new student to the class by making her feel more accepted and "connected" in a new environment. Darnell, in contrast, violated a class code with his highly audible response to the message on his phone after it rang during class. Yet his personification of the phone as a proxy listener to his reprimand for the call coming at an inopportune time was also an instance that revealed something about the material intelligence designed into the phone. It offered differing ways of interacting with and differing associated meanings of the physical device for its user as well as for others who, by their proximity, became part of the communicative situation.

There are varying possibilities as well as potential problems for learning linked to the material intelligence designed into digital devices. According to Gee (2004), the thinking, problem solving, and knowledge "stored" in digital media can help learners to combine "the results of their own thinking . . . [with the material intelligence] to achieve yet more powerful effects" (210). In the example of Rosa's digital story, it was clear that aspects of the material intelligence of the computer allowed her to "give voice" to more of what she knew about the backstory to her project. With her classmates focused on her preconstructed digital story (which had its own multitextual communicative structure), she found that, despite her shyness, she was able to extend the meanings of the story she produced in a particular format with additional discussion points and answers to questions. Utilizing these kinds of affordances allowed Ms. Foster and Ms. Young to provide more choices and differentiation to tap into the variable resources, interests, and learning styles of their students. This aspect of learning is captured by the earlier student comment that the technology "gives me other options for work." In effectively connecting and building on the backgrounds and experiences of youth, the cultural competence of teachers must now extend to the microcultural affiliations that individual youth have that reveal knowledge gained from digitally mediated experiences in semiotic domains of highly specific affinity groups.

There were additional instances where student cell phones were used in concert with the overall goals of the class. For example, because there were few digital cameras available, some students used their phones to take pictures for their projects. Emma provided an interesting example of this. She had not been able to find the image that she wanted for one of the projects, so she decided to draw it. She took a picture of the drawing and sent it to her e-mail account. Then she downloaded the picture on the computer and dragged it into Photoshop to edit and merge it into her project. Emma was also one of the students who immediately began to help set up the digital cameras when they first arrived in class. She and Deja clearly did not need to read the instructions because both had some intuitive knowledge along with dispositions to probe how the devices worked. Intuitive knowledge, according to Gee (2004), is built up through repeated practice and experience with technology. Like Emma and Deja, DeShawn also had prior experiences uploading various kinds of digital texts. So he was both comfortable and somewhat competent in probing another digital environment, a blog, to figure out how to tap its capacity to host a slideshow on a "world wide wall."

These instances of ways that students were independently probing and learning to use (or reappropriating the use of) various digital devices revealed another consideration for new learning principles—the role of a "third participant." Essentially, the material intelligence designed into digital devices plays important roles in the learning dynamic through ways that it teaches us as we engage it. In other words, systematic processes for learning at differentiated levels have been designed into digital devices including multi-user virtual environments. I believe that this requires us to augment sociocultural theories of learning and considerations of concepts like the zone of proximal development. Work in Ms. Foster's class provided glimmers of ways that the material intelligence in digital media itself functions as an "expert other" (a third participant in addition to the original notion of expert and novice) to guide the development of learners through various levels of potential. Teachers must understand how to most effectively utilize this third participant, and they must also realize that it has significant potential for stimulating learning that does not depend on the physical presence of a human "expert," including a teacher. Also, as will be seen in chapter 4, on "virtual" world media, the virtual presence and interactions with other "more capable peers" online can similarly contribute to advancing learning in virtual zones of development. This is the "collective intelligence" produced through interactions of an individual with others in learning events that can be virtual or actual. Work at V-Tech provided insights into the play of both material intelligence and collective intelligence in the learning of students and teachers.

The photography, digital storytelling, blog, and podcast projects were all created by converging an array of multimodal texts as well as written texts. These convergences required the students to understand and appreciate complex, semiotic interrelations across multiple sign systems. Their learning resources, styles, and interests were aided by the multimodal nature and the material intelligence of the digital media that facilitated students actively and critically probing for and producing knowledge and meaning about the world. Yet the role of the teachers in designing and mediating activities and projects in ways that systematically guide student interactions with digital media is still paramount to the overall efficacy of the students' learning.

CHANGING TEACHING PRACTICES

Urban schools in the United States are marked by stark disparities in academic performances and disproportionate negative outcomes for particular groups of students. Although there are historically entrenched economic, political, and geographic structures that contribute to shaping school and classroom outcomes and issues, it is clear that much can be done to ameliorate approaches to teaching and learning. At V-Tech, the challenges were exceptionally intense. Students were transferred out of the traditional high school and sent to this school at any time during the year, as was highlighted in the description of a day in the life of the class. Once at V-Tech, students rarely attended consistently. In some cases, infrequent attendance was the reason a student was sent to the school in the first place. In other cases, it was because a student had adult responsibilities outside of school, like taking care of family members or needing to work long hours. This was the case of Darius, a highly motivated student who was clearly capable of excelling academically and loved music production but had to work several jobs to help his family. There were also cases of chronic mental and physical problems, like what Jalen revealed in his podcast. Sometimes, frequent absences were the result of students being caught in various processes of the juvenile incarceration system.

Transformations in schooling are needed to reengage marginalized students, but the need is just as crucial to more effectively prepare all students for the mercurial and risky global economies, dramatically changing technologies, intense contact zones of intersecting world cultures, and critical environmental conditions that demarcate life in this century. In this regard, it could be argued that most of our students are at risk. As Luke (1998) stated over a decade ago, "There is also a risk that our teaching might succeed—succeed at generating forms of reading and writing that don't have much purchase or power in New Times" (3). If we are able to change teaching practices to effectively address these challenges, we will also significantly reduce the number of marginalized students. As we rethink the learning and literacy needs of contemporary youth, we cannot merely draw linear trajectories from our own backgrounds and experiences. Like with the emergence of cell phones, earlier analog practices do not necessarily prepare people for the plethora of novel communicative possibilities that now exist. It will not be sufficient to simply reengineer models of schooling based on our own educational experiences; we need to invent new models. We can begin by scrapping dated structures of the traditional subjects that are taught.

In this concluding section, I discuss ways that the work in Ms. Foster's class informs how teaching practices can change in order to help students acquire more power and purchase in and beyond school. I also show how work in the class reflects key perspectives of the TEACH Project. First, however, I provide a brief consideration of what it is that teaching practices need to change away from, along with why the structures and cultures of U.S. schooling are so intractable. Every year, I teach a class in my university's program for English teacher preparation, and there are stark contrasts between the pedagogical perspectives of our program and the reality of teaching in many surrounding public schools. For example, while I was writing this chapter, one of the new teachers told me that the English department in his school required him to teach a whole class on grammar every day of the school year. The teacher himself felt this was a complete waste of time, and his distress in teaching this class seemed to be exceeded only by that of his students. This situation implicates the culture of a particular school, but of more concern is the pervasive structure of schooling in the United States that both permits and requires it. Changing teaching practices is ultimately tied to changing the underlying values, beliefs, and cultural models that dictate and sustain and reproduce the practices, even when they are ineffective or, worse yet, actually harming youth.

Lakoff (2004) provided an analogy for how underlying values and beliefs of traditional orientations to schooling in the United States can be conceived as a "strict father" model. The prime element of this model is that preserving and extending a conservative form of morality is the highest goal with education and other societal institutions aligned and dedicated to serving that goal. A key aspect of this construct is the need to establish obedience to a moral authority. For education to do this, its character should be that of a strict father who rewards achievement in mastering curriculum content that reflects particular values and views and who punishes and shames undisciplined students whose very failure is an indication that they are not worthy of societal benefits and rewards. Mastery is extensively assessed by testing with definitive right and wrong answers. Lakoff contrasted the strict model to a "nurturant parent" model. Prime elements of the nurturant model are empathy and responsibility. Through empathy and responsibility, a nurturing parent will try to take care of and protect youth while working to ensure that they have opportunities for fulfilled, free lives.

The essence of the change reflected in Ms. Foster's practice was in her enactment of a nurturant model of teaching and learning with her students. This contrasted markedly with the strict model that had framed her students' experiences in school before coming to V-Tech. To be sure, this nurturant model was at the core of the whole school's approach to working with students with its emphasis on relationships, rigor, and relevance. But it is significant to show how this model was enacted as the context in which Ms. Foster's students learned. It began with her and Ms. Young's willingness to do and share projects right along with their students. So, rather than the instructors' personal backgrounds and interests being apart from the class, they became a part of the class. One consistent structure for this was the daily warm-up activities in which they did things right along with the students like wrote short poems together, wrote headlines about themselves, popped balloons with personal communication prompts, and addressed questions about themselves that were generated by these activities. In a response on our survey that asked what was liked and disliked about the class, one student noted, "The thing I liked about the class was every morning when I came in here, there was positive energy."

These community builders facilitated members of the class sharing experiences and being responsible to each other as human beings in concert with sharing experiences as learners. For example, one class started with a brief game of musical chairs. At one point, a male student didn't get to a seat on time but felt that someone else had played unfairly. He quit and went over to the other side of the room. But his fellow students started encouraging him to come back in such a humorous way that it allowed him to return to the circle without losing face. In addressing the social context of classrooms, Dewey (1938) wrote, "Every experience affects for better or for worse the attitudes which help decide the quality of further experiences" (38). Ultimately, the nature of each experience in class is tied to how students feel about themselves, about each other, about their teachers, and about learning. Another response from the survey stated, "Everyone was really nice and respectful toward each other. I really enjoyed coming to class everyday. What I like about the class is that everyone got along and there wasn't any drama and people fighting."

Dance's (2002) research vividly captured how youth who live with conditions of violence are often prone to bringing postures of toughness from the streets ("being hard enough") into the school, both for protection against peers and as a way of resisting schooling practices. Yet, despite the fact that many of the students at V-Tech were assigned to the school for severe discipline issues among other things, there was not a single instance of a fight in Ms. Foster's class during the entire academic year. Instead, the "drama" was in the actual learning activities that the students felt were challenging as well as fun. Many of the survey responses reflected this, as in the following example: "We hardly did a lot of boring readings. Everything we do in this class makes me think and we have fun doing it." In addition to the excitement and challenge, students felt that the activities were relevant. One of the survey responses that reflected this noted, "I liked that we talked about real stuff instead of boring stuff that doesn't effect [sic] me." The students were given a wide range of choices in how they could approach their projects, but clear guidelines were set for the quality of work expected as well as how the work would be assessed. It was also clear that the students' genuine voices and views were welcomed in the class, even if they were sometimes strident. This was exemplified by the response of a student who "loved the energy, the discussion, the fact that we had real freedom of speech."

Ms. Foster's approach was reflective of and also shaped by central considerations that the TEACH Project promoted in professional development with all of the teachers in the school. In the first semester, the project worked with practice-based examples of the effectiveness of mediating learning through classroom discourse in the context of particular kinds of social interactions between teachers and students and among students as collaborative partners. The CREDE principles as well as principles of collegial pedagogy provided a common language and set of perspectives to explicitly delineate what the nature of these communicative and social interactions should be. So work across the teachers' classes was guided and supported with respect to ways that they were attempting to enact joint productive activities, develop students' literacy through particular projects and across disciplines, plan activities to directly build on students' prior knowledge and experiences, utilize specific instructional conversations, and make their projects both interesting and challenging by designing complex tasks for learning.

Additionally, the professional development used the issues and activities that teachers shared from their current practices to address how youth-led inquiry could be encouraged, how accountability structures for the work of students could be more effectively distributed, and how student projects could also contribute to influencing social change beyond school. Regarding this last point, Ms. Foster did a number of things with her students that went beyond the classroom that I will only briefly mention or note again like the Jena Six event conducting a workshop at a nearby university, attending a series of classes at a nearby community college on urban sociology, and taking a contingent of students to the first national Youth Bill of Rights conference as well as an American Anthropological Association conference in Washington, D.C. This group also toured black colleges in the area while in Washington.

Ms. Foster and other V-Tech teachers shared work that they were doing in their classes with their colleagues in the PD sessions, and the framework provided by this complex of teaching principles and perspectives was used both as a guide for influencing and an optic for seeing the changes in their teaching practices. The main focus of the project, however, was to facilitate these principles of effective teaching through higher levels of digital mediation of instruction. Ms. Foster indicated at one point that she felt her students were influenced more by the human aspects (the relational aspects) of the class than by the technology aspects. Yet it is clear that her holistic approach to learning through building healthy relationships among participants in the class was appreciably realized through the dynamic interactions and communications enabled by digital media. The technology also provided unique resources for virtually supporting and extending her students' learning beyond the temporal and physical limits of the classroom. In the case of Darius, who had to work to help his family, for example, Ms. Foster was able to keep him "plugged in" to the class via the Internet. He kept up with much of his class work by using computers at the local public library. Similarly, the class came to have thoughtful and, at times, intense discussions on their blogs prompted by topics that originated in class.

Ms. Foster eventually created direct links between the work in the class and specific state academic literacy standards, just as Youth Radio creates lesson plans linked to national standards based on some of its digital productions. Consequently, the principal decided that the second semester qualified as a core academic course rather than just an elective. Reporting the vibrancy and efficacy of learning and literacy in the Hip-Hop Journalism class unfortunately may be construed as needing to prove once again that these students are "worthy" to have society's benefits and rewards meted out to them. These young people are acutely aware of how they have been profiled and positioned, but as one anonymous response on our student survey aptly noted, "We are smarter than they think."

3 | DIGITAL TEACHERS

Ms. Foster's use of digital media for learning in her journalism class reflected her developing competencies to design and implement instruction in new ways. In addition to efforts of teachers, administrators, parents, and community members to create a culture of caring at V-Tech, students also needed to be engaged in a range of dynamic learning activities guided by principles of effective teaching. As illustrated in chapter 2, Ms. Foster's use of technology was ultimately in the service of more comprehensive goals for academic and social development of her students. Importantly, she was also instrumental in the development of her fellow teachers, through her willingness to try and share new things she was learning both in conjunction with the TEACH Project and via her connections to Youth Radio. In the recursive process of learning to use a variety of digital tools, for example, Ms. Foster readily volunteered her teaching experiences for review and critique regarding both the possibilities and problems that were encountered in her journalism and Spanish classes. Other teachers eventually became comfortable following Ms. Foster's lead, experimenting with new approaches to teaching using various digital tools they had learned about in professional development as well as sharing their experiences with the other teachers in subsequent sessions.

A process of teachers learning from teachers was central to our approach to professional development in the school. We agreed with Stigler and Hiebert (1999) that for teachers to significantly improve their practices, more professional opportunities were needed for them to learn on the job with and from each other. For this to happen, however, teachers needed significant time and systematic support to work and learn together. The principal committed substantial blocks of time by scheduling 90-minute PD sessions approximately every other week, and the TEACH Project provided a structured program of both guidance and support. A key aspect of the program was to focus on the actual curricular work and pedagogical challenges occurring in the participants' classrooms. Another key aspect was to structure the learning of the teachers in the PD sessions in ways that modeled approaches they could use with students in their classrooms. The project's focus was larger than just informing teachers about instructional uses of digital tools; it was also focused on helping the teachers develop a common vision and language framed by effective principles of teaching and learning as well as an understanding of how these principles could be powerfully enacted with appropriate digital tools.

From this perspective, knowledge and skill with technology are only part of what is needed for effective instruction. In my work with educators across the country, it became important to emphasize the need for teachers to continually develop four types of knowledge and associated skills: disciplinary knowledge (and proficiency with methods for creating, accessing, and synthesizing knowledge in specific disciplines); cultural knowledge (and understanding of the cultural logics that underlie situated social practices and meaning making); technological knowledge (and skills to operate and appropriate technological tools for instruction); and pedagogical knowledge (including understanding sociocultural theories of learning as well as strategies to incorporate the other three kinds of knowledge to achieve desired learning experiences and outcomes). These four areas of knowledge are intricately intertwined in teaching practices, and deliberate instructional designs for their deployment determine the quality of students' learning. The effectiveness of these instructional designs is determined by the quality of teachers' learning.

This chapter describes V-Tech teachers learning to expand their pedagogical perspectives and strategies through developing knowledge and skills in the use of digital media to more effectively incorporate the backgrounds and experiences of their students into academic learning. I begin this discussion with an example of one teacher's use of Google Earth in his math class, to illustrate the intricate connections between disciplinary, cultural, technological, and pedagogical knowledge as well as connections to CREDE standards. After that, I describe how we used the PD sessions throughout the school year to continue developing relationships and methods of professional collaboration that facilitated acquiring the teaching perspectives, strategies, and skills to more effectively mediate student learning.

MATH ON GOOGLE EARTH

One PD workshop in the spring of 2008 focused on teachers exploring Google Earth with its extensive maps, satellite images, and other tools that let users "fly" anywhere on earth to view the geography and architecture of selected sites. Mr. Guy, the math teacher, immediately saw ways to utilize this web-based tool in his class and began designing a project to develop his students' understanding of the tangent function in trigonometry. The tangent, sine, and cosine are fundamental trigonometric functions that describe relationships between the sides and angles of triangles. For a given angle in a right-angled triangle, the tangent is the trigonometric function equal to the length of the side opposite the angle, divided by the length of the adjacent side. In figure 1, Tan A = opposite/adjacent, or a/b. This figure is useful in visualizing the particular way that Mr. Guy's math project helped his students have a more tangible and meaningful experience in learning the tangent function. Essentially, the project he designed challenged his students to use Google Earth and trigonometry to calculate the height of prominent objects near their school and in their world.

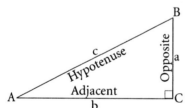

Fig. 1. Triangle

The math project had four phases that took place over two days: priming activities in the classroom to review and practice sine, cosine, and tangent functions; working in the school's computer lab to learn to use the various tools on the Google Earth website; going outside on the street to physically measure angles of prominent objects; and going back into the computer lab and then to the classroom to work on calculations to determine the height of selected objects. In the priming phase, the students reviewed concepts and problems that they had worked on with sine, cosine, and tangent functions from the past week. They had considerable background knowledge before they did the Google Earth lab project, but Mr. Guy said that he wanted to make trigonometry more immediate and personal for them by providing real-world applications and challenges.

When the students went into the computer lab for the second phase of the project, Mr. Guy gave them a lab assignment sheet that walked them through all the steps of moving around on Google Earth and using the various tools to establish and fly to coordinates, to zoom in and out on objects and sites, and to measure distances between selected coordinates. Initially, the assignment sheet directed them to nearby familiar sites; then it gave them sites and objects to find and fly to all over the world, like the Great Pyramids of Egypt and the Great Wall of China. "They played around a lot," Mr. Guy told me in an interview about the project. "Sometimes it was hard to keep them on point with the assignment because they would want to go to their friends' houses in the neighborhood or go see a nearby mall."

The last step on the computer lab assignment sheet was for the students to consider how they could use Google Earth and trigonometry to calculate the height of the flagpole on V-Tech's campus. Most of the students were able to see that the "opposite" side of a triangle like the one depicted in figure 1 could represent the flagpole and that Google Earth could be used to mark and then determine a distance for the "adjacent" side. Consequently, it was clear that if the angle at "tangent A" could be determined, they would have the values needed to use the tangent function to calculate the height of the flagpole. When they reached this stage in their reasoning, Mr. Guy showed them an altimeter and explained how it could be used to determine the tangent A angle. Afterward, he took the class outside to actually use the altimeter to get the angles for selected objects to use for their calculations of the objects' heights. One technical note is that the altimeter could also be used to determine the height of an object. To do this, however, the person using it would need to be exactly 150 meters away. So the need to be an exact distance from the object gives this way of getting the height significant limitations. Mr. Guy instead set up the project so that the students had to use trigonometric functions to make the calculations of the height, with the altimeter providing one needed value and Google Earth providing the other.

In the third phase of the project, the class went outside on the corner across the street from the school to get data on a number of prominent objects (tall buildings, clock towers, telephone poles, etc.) to take back to class and use in their calculations. The altimeter looks like a big pistol, with a trigger near the handle and a crosshair site at the tip of what looks like a barrel. It is made of bright blue plastic and would not be mistaken for a gun. Yet it is aimed like a gun, and when the trigger is pulled, it has a gauge on the side that displays the angle of the line that goes to the point at which it was aimed. As each student took a turn using the altimeter to determine the angle of a selected object, drivers slowed down to stare at the sidewalk scene. One student initially held the altimeter in an "execution style" (pointed down) but then quickly aimed it the right way. Another student talked on his cell phone as he waited in line for his turn, while another balanced on a skateboard. A bus pulled up to its stop on the corner, and its passengers peered out at Mr. Guy and his students. A couple of drivers honked their horns as they passed. At one point, a police car slowly cruised by; the officer gave a short metallic blast on the car's amplified sound system, then continued on.

In the final phase of the project, the students returned to the computer lab and eventually to the classroom to do their calculations. They were given another assignment sheet with several problems on it that reinforced the concepts needed for working out each stage of the main problem of calculating heights of objects. During this time, Mr. Guy went around the classroom and engaged small groups of students in instructional dialogues about their work. One of the considerations was the need for a correction factor based on the height of each person using the altimeter. This added a small personal dimension to the students' work.

Although Mr. Guy had a sense that using Google Earth would increase student interest in learning trigonometry, he noted that he was still "surprised to see how into it the students were." Through this project, his students understood more about the practical uses of math, rather than seeing it mainly as a school-based learning activity. Importantly, it was his disciplinary knowledge that allowed him to see specific applications of the technology to learning. He had to develop his own skills with the digital tools—his own technological knowledge. Yet it was not the nature of the tools themselves that determined their efficacy. Instead, the efficacy was in how he designed pedagogical strategies for using the tools to facilitate his students acquiring knowledge in the discipline. This pedagogical design incorporated his cultural knowledge of the students, and the project allowed them to see and visually experience something of the geometry of their lives and neighborhoods in the context of the larger world.

In this regard, Mr. Guy's approach reflected several of CREDE's principles of effective pedagogy. It engaged the students and the teacher in joint productive activities, situated academic content in contexts that were familiar to the students so that they might connect it to their prior knowledge and experiences, and used challenging, complex tasks for learning. According to Mr. Guy, "It also changed their perspective as the kids started flying around. Some of the kids have never left their neighborhoods. Now, they could fly to places like Egypt. You could see the light going on as they begin to open a bit of the global perspective."

In part, this example of math on Google Earth illustrates the significance of the role of teachers in mediating between the learner and various learning materials or tools. Other teachers in the school also found a variety of ways to enhance learning through Google Maps, like site explorations, text mapping, mapping words and places, and creating maps connected to sections of texts. I have noted earlier that because of the material intelligence in digital tools considerable learning can occur without formal assistance. However, teachers are clearly able to facilitate students interacting more productively with various materials and tools by systematically designing and guiding their learning experiences to go well beyond the direct learning they can achieve on their own.

TEACHERS' JOINT PRODUCTIVE ACTIVITY

Before becoming a university professor, I taught high school English for seven years in Chicago public schools. Perhaps the worst part of the job was attending required teacher PD workshops. Most often, a presenter would "stand and deliver" some aspect of his or her area of expertise, and teachers would endure the monologue for the allotted time. The way this corresponds to traditional structures for teaching students is not coincidental. In the TEACH Project, we wanted to support teachers in disrupting these kinds of structures that clearly have not been productive for their students. We wanted to design learning for teachers in the PD sessions in ways that modeled approaches that they also could use to activate and excite student learning in their classrooms. The first of CREDE's five standards, joint productive activity, provides an essential framework for how teachers as well as students can learn challenging content and complex skills. It suggests, along with a number of other transformational approaches, that people learn best through active, collaborative work on common goals realized through relevant learning projects. In this section, I further discuss why TEACH incorporated

CREDE, and in the following two sections, I discuss our initial work to create the "relationships" and "perspectives" that would ground our PD activities throughout the school year.

We were attracted to the CREDE standards because they were designed to transform the most fundamental relationships between teachers and students as well as between students and students. Their main focus is on shifting away from solely the teacher as the central repository of knowledge toward more collective production of knowledge and broader resources for learning. In working with these standards, it is clear that effective implementation of a given one requires significant integration of others. For example, dialogic instruction affords increased opportunity for language development, and it also affords the teacher greater understanding of the skills and interests of students, thus allowing greater contextualization to connect to students' prior knowledge in the learning of challenging content and complex tasks. In addition to the contribution of the CREDE standards to a common language and systematic set of approaches to teaching and learning, there is growing evidence of the effectiveness of implementing the standards.

A series of research studies, using both qualitative and quantitative methods, have demonstrated that students in classrooms that effectively implement CREDE standards show significant gains in reading, mathematics, and science achievement. Also, teachers' use of the standards has been positively linked to factors critical to school performance, such as motivation, perceptions, attitudes, and inclusion (Estrada and Imhoff 2001; Hilberg, Chang, and Epaloose 2003; Tharp et al. 2001; Saunders and Goldenberg 1999; Saunders et al. 1998; Stoddart 1999). Several studies recently conducted at CREDE's research and demonstration schools serving low-income Latino LEP (limited English proficiency) students showed significant positive effects of teachers' implementation of the standards on SAT 9 standardized tests and other performance measures (Doherty and Pinal 2004; Stoddart 2005). These studies demonstrate that classroom implementation of five CREDE standards is a powerful model for improving the achievement of students, particularly those at risk of academic failure.

Beyond the focus on digitally mediated learning, we wanted teachers to consciously synthesize their work around key perspectives in their educational practices, like the need for extensive collaborations with and among students on real-life projects and problems utilizing rich, dialogic language that incorporated and modeled specific disciplinary discourses. During the summer before the PD program began, members of the TEACH "core team" (I along with the principal, Ms. Foster, two graduate students, and a postdoctoral student) all participated in a two-day workshop on implementing CREDE standards that was conducted by several highly experienced CREDE trainers. A number of members of the TEACH Project also met during the summer before the implementation to discuss various scholarly works that helped us develop our approach in terms of the kinds of new models and new language that we felt would be needed to transform learning. Just before the fall semester began, the core team created a blueprint for the sequence of PD activities to be implemented over the coming academic year. These and other activities were important for the knowledge gained, the planning that was completed, and the initial forming of relationships with each other as we came together to engage in joint productive PD activities.

BUILDING RELATIONSHIPS

Thus far, I have discussed three of the V-Tech teachers: Ms. Glide, Ms. Foster, and Mr. Guy. Ms. Glide (an English teacher) and Ms. Foster (the Spanish and journalism teacher) are African American, and Mr. Guy (a math teacher) is white. They worked on professional development in the TEACH Project with five other teachers: Ms. Church (an African American who taught English), Ms. Kim (a Korean American who also taught English), Ms. Rivers (an African American who taught social studies), Mr. Roy (an African American who taught science), and Mr. Elder (an African American who taught math). As noted earlier, all but two of these teachers were under 35 years old. They were all recruited by the principal, a 41-year-old Latino, during his first two years at the school. This immediately preceded the academic year during which the TEACH Project took place. So all of the educators at the school were relatively new.

In chapter 1, I noted the importance advocated by Dewey (1938) and many others of building on student experiences for learning. We felt it was just as important to source the experiences of teachers for their learning. This perspective already existed in the school's focus, and we used the same focus of relationships, rigor, and relevance to guide our PD activities. Ms. Kim and Ms. Church volunteered their classrooms for the initial PD sessions, and when the computer lab was completed later in the first semester, the sessions then took place there. The first PD session, on September 7, 2007, was devoted to continuing the development of our relationships with each other as we also worked on consensus for our goals for the school year. We moved the desks in a circle and faced each other as we talked in our first formal session. I began by framing the context of our work together with the following statement:

> What we are trying to do is actually synthesize all the things that go into the learning outcomes for the students. These kids have kind of been cast off. We understand that there is a much more complicated set of circumstances. Yet the most important thing is the teaching. With the whole notion of V-Tech being able to continue its development using more digital mediation, we are in a position to create a model . . . where resources from the university, the community, parents, teachers, and students can come together around the same set of goals.
>
> That's kind of our overall vision, and what we would like to do in the context of teacher professional development—and we will talk a little more about this—is use this session to sort of get ideas from you guys about the kinds of things you might see being able to be supported in. At the same time, we can talk about some of the kinds of things that we [the TEACH core team] have been developing that we think might have a place once we see how all of these things can be synthesized.

I shared what the core team was initially proposing for possible PD activities during the first semester including learning about and implementing CREDE standards, developing activity centers, providing demonstration lessons on effective teaching strategies, teachers presenting to each other on the progress of their work, and trips to successful youth organizations like Youth Radio. After these PD experiences, we would then get more directly involved in learning to use various digital tools in teaching.

I asked the teachers present if the graduate students working with the project could meet with them individually some time before the next PD session to get a more in-depth sense of the teachers' ideas and desires for what could be accomplished in our collaboration, and they all agreed. We wanted to make sure that the teachers' voices were heard (though they might not speak out in the whole group) and that their particular desires for development were recognized and incorporated into the PD activities. I also talked a bit more about how this effort drew a page or two from an earlier university/school research collaboration that I had been one of the principal investigators for at the comprehensive high school that sends students to V-Tech. I noted how we could have a much higher level of impact at V-Tech with our concentrated effort on 100 to 150 students in contrast to the much larger student body of more than 3,000 students at the other school. I closed by talking briefly about my own background, including my experiences as a high school English teacher in the Chicago public schools.

For the rest of this first meeting, each teacher, the graduate students, the postdoctoral student, and the principal shared things about their backgrounds and what brought them to teaching along with their ideas for our work together. We found that we had much in common. I will give a sense of the backgrounds and goals of the teachers and the principal through their own voices. Mr. Roy, the science teacher, volunteered to talk first. "I'll just get it out the way," he began. He had received his teaching credential in the previous year, and he talked about how he was always interested in supporting youth development. Initially, he had done quite a bit of informal volunteer work in schools before becoming a teacher. "I used to do a lot of just dropping in on schools to help out. It was nothing formal," he said, observing,

> I saw a lot of students of color doing really, really bad in school—just really bad. I received no encouragement from my family whatsoever about returning to [teach] school. As a matter of fact, they still laugh at me. Things like "You were helping out kids more before you were a teacher"— they were saying things like that. And my dad was like, "You ain't gonna make no money." You know, other cultures, they come here and they knock out the economic thing first. Then they send their kids to school for real degrees—engineering, medicine, and things like that.
>
> The only reason I overcame all of that was I started subbing [at the comprehensive high school], and the kids just wanted me [to be a teacher there]. It was a lot easier for me there than here. There was this whole big thing and the administration wouldn't hire me, and the kids signed all kinds of petitions. But when I actually started teaching here, I saw that there was a big gap between where I was and where I wanted to be. I don't have no background with professional development. So I'm here, and I'm ready to work.

Interestingly, Ms. Kim, a Korean American, had the kind of immigrant experience that Mr. Roy alluded to, but it was more complicated than it appeared on the surface. This became clear as she talked about why she came to work at V-Tech: "I grew up in LA, and it's interesting because I identify with struggle because my parents have struggled even though I grew up in a middle-class house." She talked about wanting be a teacher to serve the kind of community that she can identify with because education is so important for increasing opportunities. Ms. Kim received her bachelor's and master's degrees and teaching credential from Stanford, but she noted how she felt "a little lost" there, especially during the first couple of years because so many of the students were from such wealthy backgrounds. "Most of my friends are actually immigrants or their parents are immigrants, and I feel like that immigrant experience is so central to my life. I can't really identify with people who haven't had those kinds of experiences." She said a bit more to clarify what she meant.

> I never had to worry about what I was going to eat. I never had to worry about money really. But my parents just worked every day of the year. I would go into the store and help them work on the weekends. And even though I, like, never needed anything, it was always in the back of my mind and in my parents mind that, oh, we should hang dry the clothes so that we don't have to use up energy with the dryers, and we can save on the electric bills. It's these random little things that I learn from my husband that other people don't even worry about. Like he uses a paper towel to wipe things up, and I will be, like, use a cloth that you can wash . . . you know, to save money. I just realized that there are a lot of people who don't have to ever worry about those kinds of things.
>
> In college I lived in a co-op to save money. We had to cook for everybody and clean the bathrooms, but it was also a real life-changing experience for me and just realizing all of this about class and how my parents experience influenced my own experience. The funny thing is that my parent's culture is really all about, like, becoming a lawyer or a doctor, and instead . . . I became a teacher. So that's one of their disappointments since I was the high achiever of the three children they had. But I chose to become a teacher because I don't want to be one of those people who is disconnected from their roots and what they've been through.

These considerations of being able to identify with the experiences of their students and wanting to use education as a vehicle to help transform their lives were dramatically reflected in the principal's story also. "My perspectives as an administrator come from my own experiences in school," he told us. "I got kicked out of high school when I was 16, and . . . I cannot recall a single person that not only would advocate for me but would advocate for Latino boys in general." He went on to tell us that neither of his two siblings finished high school and that his mother did not finish either, after having her first child at 15. Then he shared the following:

> We are not the family that came across the border at four in the morning, and nobody spoke English. My family has been here for generations. I think there is just this expectation, you know, of poverty. I think we came to think that this was just what was expected. . . . And when you see a 16-year-old rapper on a yacht with eight bottles of champagne, I can identify with that. And you kind of grow up with this mentality that you want to go from here to there, but not go through all the steps in between.
>
> So I don't want one Ms. Foster or one Mr. Roy; I want, like, 50 of both of them. I want to build this program . . . , and I want the students to feel good about this school. But the shadow of [the comprehensive high school] is pretty broad. We still get students now who don't want to put V-Tech on their job applications. People at the district look at my requests [for resources] and say, "You have enough, so just stop." They question why we need tech equipment when this school hasn't needed anything like this for, like, the last ten years. Unlike my staff, I'm exhausted right now. . . . This is becoming like therapy. I need all the gods to help me and give me some strength. Anyhow, I will be back here next Friday—on the couch.

There were echoes of these kinds of considerations in what other participants shared. Ms. Rivers, who teaches social studies, noted, however, that being hired to work at V-Tech this year brought her teaching career back to life. She noted that she had just about burned out teaching in a difficult urban school district not far away: "I didn't know that something you loved so much could hurt so much." With a nod to the principal, she said, "An angel brought me here." Teachers also talked about other positive aspects of the school as well as their desire to learn to use more technology in the coming year. Ms. Foster noted that the students bring such positive energy and how she's excited to begin working with Ms. Young to help with the tech piece. For her Spanish class, she wondered what it would be like to use Second Life "so that we can go to other countries to speak Spanish and go all around the world." Ms. Church, the English teacher who is in her second year at V-Tech, talked about her enthusiasm to try out some of the many ideas received in a summer workshop of the Bay Area Writing Project. She also noted,

> In terms of technology, I do want to collaborate on how to use what students are already using outside of class, especially the Sidekicks [cell

phones]. If there was a way to use the Sidekicks for some sort of assignment, then that would be a dream come true. And I'm also thinking of doing, I don't know when, but I want to do some kind of blog to have them write. I just think it would be a good idea to get them on the computer and to get their stuff out there to get some type of recognition from outside the school. I'm not sure about the topic yet. But we're going to be talking about education and equality.

The teachers and principal shared both excitement and frustration in working at the school. Teachers like Ms. Church and Ms. Foster noted that they had already been thinking about ways to incorporate more technology into their teaching, like using blogs for wider publication of student writing or using Second Life for Spanish conversations with people around the world. Ms. Church also wondered about pedagogical possibilities for cell phones. All of the teachers indicated at least a willingness to try something new. They also identified structural and institutional constraints on their desires to provide rigorous and relevant learning experiences for the students. Clearly, there were many actions of the comprehensive high school that indicated they didn't really want V-Tech to succeed academically with its students. For decades as a continuation school, it had been operated essentially as a containment space for students that the main school did not want to deal with. Some teachers and counselors at the main high school have indicated that students there actually got profiled as "looking like he belongs at V-Tech," and as a result of relatively minor infractions, the main school's administration could force involuntary transfer of students at any time during the school year.

The earlier positioning of V-Tech as a continuation high school was a consequence of a pedagogy of poverty and its normalization of failure stemming from low expectations for certain students and, in some cases, fear of them. Added to this was an absence of a wider range of pedagogical options. Consequently, the school's demographic makeup is not coincidental. Rather, it is a reflection of rigidly tracked and intractable structures of inequality that may not be significantly countered by something like a well-intentioned PD program. The other side of that argument, however, is that a setting like V-Tech's with its visionary leadership and committed teachers and staff, could be highly viable for achieving significant social and academic development with its students. These educators certainly understood key challenges their students face.

A couple of decades earlier, the principal himself might have been one of these students. So our work together on the project was an attempt to affirm the latter argument—that opportunities for learning could be created that didn't merely compensate for the schooling practices these students had been pushed out of. Instead, learning at V-Tech could model more productive and relevant ways for all students to learn in school.

Additional PD sessions during the fall semester focused on developing teaching perspectives that utilized CREDE principles as a beginning framework and language for synthesizing practices across disciplines. As we moved toward winter, the focus of the sessions shifted to the teachers actually learning to use an array of digital tools. As we moved toward spring, the sessions extended a focus on teachers learning to incorporate guidance and support for their attempts to teach with and through various digital technologies. As we moved toward summer, opportunities were provided for teachers to reflect on what they had learned and how they had put their learning into practice along with how these experiences might shape their approaches to teaching in the next academic year.

DEVELOPING PERSPECTIVES

In the second PD session of September 2008, we continued building relationships between the teachers and the university participants through activities designed to further ground us in understanding and implementing CREDE standards. We reviewed the standards and looked at several examples from CREDE documents that showed how they had been implemented in teaching practices. The examples showed how to plan with students, how to use their prior knowledge, how to make lessons meaningful, how to design group work, and how to engage students in dialogues with the teacher and other students to significantly increase student talk in the learning process. We talked about how students themselves could become more expert to also facilitate the growth of fellow students and referred to examples of young people's work at Youth Radio. I noted that I would do a demonstration lesson in the first PD session in October to further illustrate ways that the standards could be revealed in instruction.

We then formed five dyads—each composed of a teacher and a university researcher—to discuss individual standards from the standpoint of how each could be actualized (or more fully actualized) in V-Tech teachers' current practices. I paired with Ms. Church, and we talked about how the project of creating multitextual personal profiles in which her students created and documented something that was integral to who they were could be used early in the semester to establish and share more of the students' backgrounds and experiences. The graduate students in my urban education class were doing a similar project, and Ms. Church and I talked about how writing letters describing the completed projects could also be a way to initiate a writing exchange between my graduate students and her high school students. She and I decided that we would do a series of four writing exchanges to give both groups of students real audiences and genuine motivations for writing. Ms. Church and I felt that the projects would also encourage our students to experiment with making meaning using multiple textual modes as they learned what they needed to know to accomplish the objectives of the project.

When we reported back to the whole PD group, Ms. Church talked about how we saw these projects in and between our classes as a form of joint productive activity. Ms. Church also noted how her task of responding to each student's essays could be improved as a result of the graduate students writing extensive, specific responses to her students' writing in their exchanges. She saw that this would ultimately help her students prepare both for the writing portion of the high school exit exam and for any college application letters they would write.

Participants in the other dyads also reported to the whole group on how the standard they were assigned to discuss reflected or could reflect something occurring in each teacher's actual classroom. Ms. Kim shared her dyad's discussion of ways to plan some of her class activities together with her students. "I have very structured assignments," she reported, "but I'm now going to try to open them up a bit for more student input." Mr. Roy shared his dyad's discussion of ways to effectively design group work. He had struggled with discipline issues in his science classes as well as with keeping his students on task, and he reported that working in groups sometimes helped: "In small groups the kids worked to keep each other in line and focused on the work. There were cases when the students received each other even better than they received me."

Ms. Rivers reported that in discussing with her dyad partner how to keep her class activities as challenging as possible the importance of the overall design of the instruction became key. She shared a successful curricular design, focused around the refugee experience that she had implemented in her social studies class. "First, they had to brainstorm about leaving home," she told us. She then provided more details.

What it is like to leave home even if it is a positive experience. They had to consider what they were going to take with them and what they would leave behind and why. Then they read a work of fiction on the refugee experience. Then they wrote an essay where they had to make connections with the reading, their notes, and considerations of geography that we also went through. Next, we are going to go into globalization and segue right into that while still focused on the same theme.

Linking CREDE standards to work in the teachers' classes and continuing to get to know each other individually while learning from each other were how we attempted to develop core perspectives and common language for our work during the school year. In our second PD session, after teachers reported on their dyad discussions I passed out typed comments summarizing individual conversations that I or my graduate students had with them since the previous PD session. As mentioned earlier, this was to be sure that the teachers' voices were heard regarding their specific desires for professional development that they may not have verbally expressed to the whole group.

Ms. Kim's comments indicated that she was very interested in either bringing in teachers who did good work or even going to see them teach in their classrooms. She also noted that although she had significant training in project-based learning in her teacher preparations program, she was not yet doing it very much in her classes. Ms. Church's comments indicated that she liked the idea of planning together in the PD sessions and maybe doing more interdisciplinary projects—for example, between social studies and English. She also indicated a desire for the sessions to help her keep informed on new forms of technology integration into schooling, like work going on in a few places to develop curriculum that utilizes design principles of video games.

Mr. Roy's comments indicated that he liked the idea of working directly with other teachers to get help on incorporating technology into his science curriculum. He also noted that he would like to be able to take his students to UC Berkeley to sit in on college-level science classes. He did not want to see another PD program begin with good intentions and then be gone by the middle of the year. Ms. Rivers's comments echoed the need to go beyond the walls of the school on field trips. She also wanted to learn additional techniques to make her classes more interactive, including learning about the viability of educational games. She thought educational games would be interesting for her students, but she noted that she personally shied away from using technology in her teaching.

DEMONSTRATION LESSONS

In our third PD session, which occurred at the beginning of October 2008, I presented an initial demonstration lesson. Its purpose was to illustrate how a number of the CREDE standards could be utilized in instruction. Specifically, I wanted to model strategies for how teachers could access and utilize their students' prior knowledge to make learning more meaningful and for how to engage students in dialogues with the teacher and with each other to increase student talk and idea generation about academic topics. The term *idea* is here used to refer to each view held by the learner that includes visual, analogical, and mathematical views as well as descriptive views.

I also wanted the teachers to see the viability of using a variety of teaching tools and textual mediums to increase opportunities for their students to become engaged in talk about ideas. One central set of teaching tools was the collection of Thinking Maps developed by Dr. David Hyerle to facilitate teacher and student thinking. There are eight Thinking Maps that are visual tools for accessing eight distinct cognitive processes, and I employed four of them in this demonstration lesson: the circle map, for defining in context; the flow map, for sequencing; the multi-flow map, for showing cause and effect; and the double bubble map, for comparing and contrasting (see fig. 2). These maps are used extensively in the professional development of educators that is conducted around the United States by the National Urban Alliance for Effective Education.

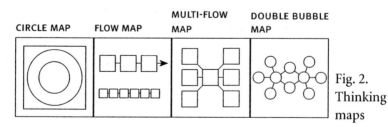

Fig. 2. Thinking maps

Finally, I wanted to model how the V-Tech teachers could use the PD sessions to pilot their developing curriculum designs in order to get ideas and input from fellow teachers and university participants. In this regard, the teachers' presentations of lessons could be more informal than my demonstration. My goal was to formally take the teachers through a process to show how particular strategies could be utilized to help students increase the quality and sophistication of their thinking and writing. I positioned the V-Tech teachers as students in this demonstration lesson, so that they could experience the strategies the way their students might experience them in their classrooms.

I built the lesson around the theme of discipline and used Robert Hayden's six-stanza poem entitled "The Whipping" as the central text. First, I asked the teachers to write the word *discipline* in the center circle of a circle map, which is used for defining in context by brainstorming ideas from prior knowledge. I next asked the teachers to write in the larger circle all the words, ideas, or beliefs that defined or were associated with this word in their minds. Then I asked for several volunteers to read what they wrote out loud, and I wrote their ideas on the board. We immediately noticed ideas we shared as well as new ideas that we had not individually considered about the word *discipline.* Next, I asked the teachers to think about where their ideas about discipline came from and to write the sources inside the square frame of the circle map; they were using the frame to identify the sources of the information they had already provided in the large circle. In this way, they had to explore and make explicit some of the social and cultural contexts that framed their ideas about the theme. Again, volunteers read and I recorded on the board the additional ideas that this part of the process had generated.

Next, I played 30-second clips from three songs that revealed very different takes on approaches to discipline: Luther Vandross's "Dance with My Father," James Brown's "Papa Don't Take No Mess," and Tupac Shakur's "Dear Mama." The purpose here was to extend the strategy involved in using the visual text of the map to musical texts that also offered ideas and perspectives about the theme of discipline. A short, lively discussion of these clips generated more ideas about discipline, and as additional ideas came up I recorded them on the board.

After these priming activities, I passed out copies of "The Whipping" and asked for a volunteer to read the poem out loud. I asked the teachers to use a flow map to record what happened in the poem—just the sequence of events. At this point, Ms. Kim stated, "I don't understand the difference between what we are doing now with the flow map and what we did before." Rather than attempting to give an immediate answer, I asked her to go through this step to experience what happens. She decided to work with Mr. Roy to map the sequence of events, and they had an animated discussion as they tried to come to consensus. After the teachers finished this activity, volunteers were asked to read the sequence that they had mapped. We noted key differences in the way the poem was mapped by different teachers. We discussed the differences and went back and forth with the text of the poem itself in order to come to agreement on an accurate rendering of the sequence of events that Hayden had described. Ms. Church told the group that using the flow map had substantially changed her interpretation of the poem. She said, "Having to get things into the boxes pushed me to isolate different occurrences in ways that helped me more clearly see their relationship to each other."

The teachers quickly realized that many of the differences in their accounts were tied to the fact that they had included their own interpretations of the meaning of the poem rather than just describing the events that had occurred. After this consideration was established, I had the teachers use a multi-flow map as an aid to further expand and concretize their interpretations. This map was designed to elicit cause-and-effect relationships, and by putting the word *whipping* in the center box, the teachers were able to see how they could generate ideas from textual evidence in the poem that contributed to the cause of the whipping in contrast to ideas based on textual evidence that could be connected to effects or consequences of the whipping. Essentially, this process offered a way to systematically extend interpretations based on textual evidence that could also be compared to other emerging interpretations depicted in the multi-flow maps of other members of the group. When the teachers were finally able to engage a more open interpretative discussion of the poem, it had the effect of sourcing all of the ideas that had been generated and expanded from the various multimodal prompts, actively sorting and evaluating those ideas based on justifications from actual textual evidence, and thereby enabling participants to synthesize the best ideas from all sources into an integrated understanding of the poem. The discussion of the possible meanings of the poem was quite lively, but it was also at a high level of interpretative sophistication, and the ameliorative roles that the various prompts had played was apparent.

Next, I passed out a copy of a single page from Alice Walker's *The Color Purple* on which Celie talks to Harpo about marriage and also describes how her husband had treated her: "He beat me like he beat the children." I asked the teachers to use a double bubble map to create a visual documentation of the points of comparison and contrast between the two texts. More ideas around the issues surrounding discipline that came up in this part of the discussion were recorded on the board. Finally, I showed a four-minute clip from the movie *Glory* in which the black Civil War soldier played by Denzel Washington is punished with a public whipping. We concluded our discussion of the theme with additional ideas that were generated by this provocative video text and completed the recording of ideas on the board.

I ended the demonstration lesson by passing out copies of two well-developed argumentative essays written by seventh-grade students in a public school in Newark, New Jersey, who I had taught this same lesson to. These two essays were examples of the arguments that had been written by all of the students in that class on propositions surrounding corporal punishment. One essay argued for and the other against the use of corporal punishment. I discussed how both essays reflected ways that the individual students had taken ownership of a number of ideas that had been generated through use of the different texts and through the various discussions about the expanding considerations of the theme of discipline and punishment. I illustrated how their essays incorporated some of these ideas into their arguments whether the arguments were for or against the proposition. In essence, these students had been able to take advantage of the collective intelligence of their class and draw on a wide range of ideas that had been generated in a variety of textual mediums. In the process of the lesson, the emerging ideas were recorded in a number of ways that could be easily accessed and reviewed. I also discussed how working with students to build a repertoire of ideas could reveal the development of their processes of individual and collective meaning making from initially generating, to sorting, to evaluating ideas in the development of more highly integrated knowledge about topics.

Because they had actually experienced them, the V-Tech teachers could clearly see the viability of the mutitextual and multimodal strategies for making text-to-self, text-to-text, and text-to-world connections and how the strategies facilitated higher levels of student talk and learning from other students' ideas through planned, goal-directed dialogues. They talked about how the tools could help students more clearly see complex aspects of an academic text, like the way our mapping of the events of the poem also forced a discussion about the narrator and the narrator's role in the poem in contrast to that of the author. Ms. Church noted on this point, "I haven't been able to see students bring in the role of the narrator in defining the overall meaning of a poem, and I think this approach would help them with that." We also discussed how this process allowed for learning to take place even when some ideas that were generated were obviously incorrect. As the principal chimed in, "The bad ideas might be as good for learning as the good ideas." The participants also could see the critical but transformed role of the teacher as the designer and guide for challenging and engaging activities to stimulate complex thinking and motivate more sophisticated writing. They also discussed the utility of these approaches for other academic disciplines beyond language arts and how elements of approaches like this were already going on in some classes. For example, Ms. Church drew our attention to a graphic organizer posted on the wall in the classroom we were then using that Ms. Kim had created to help students organize and generate ideas for writing.

In subsequent PD meetings, other teachers volunteered to present their emerging designs for lessons to inform the group and to get our responses and insights. Mr. Roy's first presentation of a lesson idea was interesting because it also revealed limits to the usefulness of our responses when the focus went beyond the collective disciplinary knowledge of the group. He had written topics and ideas on the board for three of his upcoming science units. He began by giving us a handout and talking about how he had been thinking about teaching the units: "Before we start with anything, I always have warm-ups that have something to do with science. For example, this sheet I gave you has health facts on precursors to diabetes." The third unit was on cells and genetics, and Mr. Roy told us, "That's the one that I was going to ask for some help with because I felt like I could put some culture into it, because I got some ideas from our session last time. There's not a lot of culture in the textbook." He showed us a copy of a thick, new science textbook. Then he added, "I've been working on it. I'm just having a real struggle with many of my students to have them really get into it with science." He talked a bit more about specific activities he was considering and about how he eventually hoped to use some kind of technology in the class. He also talked about problems he was having getting adequate lab supplies. He closed by saying, "So now I'm just going to sit down and listen to all of your ideas about how you can help me."

There was silence for a while as we all tried to think of ways to help

Mr. Roy develop his lesson. Finally, Ms. Kim, who has been thumbing through the science textbook, said, "Yeah, this book is a little intimidating. I think because I haven't had to look at a book like this in so many years, and I'm saying, like, wow, there is so much information on each page." Mr. Roy responded, "And that's intimidating for a lot of our students. They see this book and say, 'What?' and they just shut down. They look at all of these words and say, 'Man, I got to outline all of this.' And that's why I'm trying to rethink how to approach things." One of the graduate students offered a suggestion. "You could set up your activity center stuff and have the students use the book as a reference. If you talked about how some prisoners are being exonerated through DNA evidence, maybe some of these men would come to class, you could link that to genetics, and this might be able to hook kids on the science of it." This seemed to be an interesting suggestion, and other teachers offered additional suggestions. Yet it was clear that Mr. Roy did not feel that much of what was being offered could really help him with the overall challenges that he faced in his classes. He was the only science teacher in the school, and our lack of knowledge of his discipline mitigated our collective abilities to offer strategies to significantly help him transform his teaching during the first semester of the school year.

ACTIVITY CENTERS

Despite not being able to support every teacher to the extent that was needed, the structure of having teachers respond to the work of other teachers was an important part of our PD approach. It allowed us to keep the focus for teacher learning on actual work that they were doing in their classrooms. This approach worked well during the first semester, when the focus was on developing teaching perspectives and practices that would also be central to the teachers' more direct learning of digital mediation strategies in the second semester. The final component that we felt was critical to teaching with technology was the use of activity centers. Organizing classrooms into activity centers (or learning stations) transforms the fundamental structure of teaching and learning by making it possible for teachers to responsively instruct and assist small groups of students. The CREDE approach advocates the use of activity centers as the most effective way to incorporate and realize its standards for effective pedagogy in the actual practices of teaching and learning (Hilberg, Chang, and Epaloose 2003).

Ms. Foster, as noted earlier, was not only an effective teacher; she was also a teacher leader in the school. When we focused on activity centers in the PD sessions during the first semester, she took the lead in planning and eventually modeling their use in her Spanish classes. In the last PD session in October, she volunteered to present a lesson plan for a unit that would utilize activity centers in order to get suggestions from the group before implementing it. Like Mr. Roy, she began by putting a number of her ideas for the unit on the board while also talking about some of the background considerations surrounding the unit. "There are all these different versions of how death is dealt with," she said. "There is the Hollywood version; there are different cultural ways. I still haven't started this yet, so are there any ideas how I can do this? I'm still trying to finish up the last lesson." The teachers offered suggestions, and as they did, she wrote their ideas on the board.

The unit would have students researching and creating projects in Spanish on how different cultures deal with death. Some of the goals for the unit were to have students understand differences in how people look at and experience death; to document healthy ways of expressing death and other things associated with it orally, in writing, and in other textual mediums; and finally to explore ways to help stop community violence. As with most of the PD sessions, the principal was present, and he responded to Ms. Foster's ideas by saying, "The centers are just supposed to be a part of this. If we can hone in with you, Ms. Foster, on the three or four things that you want them to have as products at the end of the curriculum cycle, it would clarify the nature of the centers and what kinds of activities should go on at them." "I saw this as a two-week experience," Ms. Foster responded. "The writing assignments are a poem, a composition. I see a poetry center, a history center, and a Silence the Violence one, and also some sort of altar. I'm thinking about something where students take pictures. I'm not exactly sure what to do with this, but it might be the culminating activity for a center." "You could put a whole bunch of pictures on the floor, and everyone walks around and then picks up a picture and then just talks about it in Spanish," said Ms. Church. "Do we break out and look at each center, or do we do it in a whole group?" Mr. Roy asked. "We can throw out a bunch of ideas, and then you keep what sticks," said the principal. "I have an idea for the poetry center," said Ms. Kim. "It could be a place where they go to read poetry and then translate it into writing. The reading can be translated by writing it in Spanish."

The principal then noted, "Ms. Foster brought her plan to the group, and it just hit me that elements of her plan were already organizers for the various learning stations." He stated further, "The idea is that once you set these centers up, students should not have to come back to you and say what should I be doing at this center. I was also going to suggest a technology center." "Everyone knows by now that the ten laptops on our mobile computer lab have been stolen," Ms. Foster said, choking back emotion. "That's why it's hard to end the current unit because my students' had PowerPoint presentations on those laptops. My ideal was to have a laptop at each learning station so that there may be times when students go to a computer just to do research for their project." [After the theft, as noted in chapter 2, the principal decided to dedicate one classroom as a secure computer lab and to place new iMac computers he had purchased there rather than on mobile carts.] Ms. Foster continued to talk about things she had recently done to partially address the impact of the theft of the laptops on her students. "I had all of my students get Gmail accounts," she said. "You can create documents within Gmail, so you can access all of your PowerPoints online. That way we don't have to worry about our work being lost again. I also created a blog for each of my classes, so all of my assignments are online. All this has been really helpful, and it couldn't have come at a better time." By the end of this PD session, Ms. Foster had decided on creating four activity centers: one for building an altar; a poetry and translations center; one for writing and vocabulary; and one for viewing, talking about, and making photographs, pictures, and other visual texts.

LEARNING TO USE DIGITAL TOOLS

Although Ms. Foster had already been using technology in the Hip Hop Journalism class and to a lesser extent in her Spanish classes during the fall semester, she was an anomaly among the V-Tech teachers in this regard. The TEACH Project's goal was to facilitate all of the teachers becoming competent in incorporating more technology in teaching. The work of the first semester on building relationships and developing teacher knowledge and perspectives regarding effective teaching practices through a process of joint activities was important to creating the framework within which the teachers actually learned to use and eventually would teach by using a variety of digital tools. As we moved toward the end of the fall and into the second semester, we focused the PD sessions directly on guiding and supporting teachers in learning how to use a range of digital media in their teaching.

In making this transition, the TEACH Project hired a technology specialist, Mr. Cameron, to work with the core team to plan the second semester of professional development and to lead the sessions. The title for his position was Director of Instructional Technology. The principal had the expertise to lead these sessions himself; he has been the director of technology and instruction for schools on the East Coast. But he contributed his vision and support for the effort through his role as a member of the core team that was providing the primary structure during this school year for teachers to transition from novice to more expert users of technology in their classrooms. We were particularly excited about Mr. Cameron working with us because he had done similar work in Chicago in a technology project that worked both in the public schools and in nonprofit community and youth organizations. We had looked to that project to learn about some of the innovative things being done that could help us think both imaginatively and pragmatically about our work in California. He was also a graduate student in the School of Information Sciences at the University of California, Berkeley, and I had been influenced in the development of the TEACH Project by Peter Lyman, a professor in that school, as well as the work of the Digital Youth Project that he guided.

In the first PD session of January 2008, the principal formally introduced Mr. Cameron to V-Tech teachers and staff. The principal invited the support staff to this session because he wanted them to also be attuned to new ways that students in the school may be engaging in learning. For example, there might be times when students were in the school's computer lab after class working on assigned projects, and he wanted staff members to see these activities as legitimate work even if it might initially look like the students were just listening to music on the computers. In the following statement, the principal drew on the design of a new elective class that was going to be offered to talk about how he saw professional development working for the rest of the year.

> One of the things I'm excited about with this new class is that the instructor didn't just talk about an individual computer program or application

in isolation, but about creating a product that encompasses several or many applications at one time to achieve a desired effect. This is the way that designers think. It's not like I just have this one application, so I'm restricted to that. It's like what's the end thing I want to create and what's available to me to do those things. That's also what we have in mind with these workshops. Mr. Cameron doesn't see these as individual workshops where you learn about isolated applications like a podcast or a blog. It's really about imagining the kinds of things you want students to create and thinking about the design and intersection of the kinds of applications that will allow them to do these things.

After these introductory remarks, the principal turned the session over to Mr. Cameron. "I'm really glad you brought that up," he began, "because that's exactly what I was going to bring up. He then talked about how he saw his role in his position.

I'm a bit apprehensive with the title you all gave me—particularly with the word *technology,* because the technology is just one part of it. . . . The focus for me is not to bring in more [technical] complexity, but for us to really think about what learning consists of. How do we approach teaching in terms of what's not a waste of time for us and not a waste of time for our students. . . . So it's more about us rethinking and reframing our work as teachers. That's how I see my work here. . . . We will introduce some themes and ideas. We will learn about some tools to help us explore, or expand, or present those ideas. Then you all can experiment with actually doing things in your classrooms and come back to the next session, and hopefully some of you will volunteer to talk about what you did and how it went, or even talk about how you just thought about doing it in your classroom. . . . And I will be available during the week to come to your classrooms to help out with projects that you all may be doing.

Mr. Cameron was clearly attempting to put the teachers at ease about what was going to happen in the coming PD sessions. Essentially, he presented the framework that had been developed in conjunction with the core team to integrate the learning of a number of digital tools with actual work going on in the teachers' classrooms but to keep it mainly at a low-stakes, voluntary level in terms of expectations of the teachers doing specific things in their classrooms. We wanted the learning activities not to be intimidating or stressful for the teachers, yet the final design for the second semester was quite comprehensive covering podcasting, blogging, various Google applications, digital photography and video, storyboarding with Comic Life, and explorations of Second Life, in that order. Mr. Cameron's work on the development and implementation of the design was critical, and eventually he mainly met with the principal and me before or after a session to review or revise things. I will give a brief overview to show the coherence of the sequence of activities and then provide additional descriptions of ways the teachers were engaged in learning about these media.

The second semester of professional development began with the teachers learning how to create podcasts using GarageBand. A podcast is an audio recording that can be manipulated (remixed) using an application like GarageBand to create a variety of verbal, musical, and other sound as well as visual effects. The reason for starting with podcasting was to give the teachers an initial experience with a relatively simple form of digital media that they could immediately use to bring their students' voices and perspectives into the curriculum through audio recordings, by having them interview each other or family and community members, by tying this to class projects, and by posting the podcasts to websites online.

The next phase of the sessions was focused on having the teachers post to blogs and eventually create their own blogs during subsequent sessions. As a personal publishing platform, the blog offered additional tools for the teachers to use to manage, manipulate, and publish information of their own and from their students. The teachers learned how to do simple text postings as well as how to utilize more sophisticated features like adding pictures, creating thematic categories for hosting different conversations, or even uploading podcasts that they or their students had recorded. Mr. Cameron created a V-Tech blog for the PD sessions and encouraged the teachers to continually use it for comments about things they were trying out in their classes as well as for periodic reflections on their experiences with other aspects of the professional development. Another thing he initiated early on was to have the teachers draw designs or floor plans of how they would physically arrange their classrooms to most effectively accommodate digital learning. This connected to and extended the work of the first semester on the design and use of activity centers. Later in the second semester, some of the PD sessions themselves were structured around activity centers that had different foci for the work at each one, like a center for working on blogs, or one for working on podcasts, or one for working on digital graphics and photography.

As the work with podcasts and blogs continued to thread through and become more elaborated in subsequent PD sessions, the functions of Google Maps, Google Documents, and Google Images were introduced. The teachers learned how to connect the visual imaging capabilities of the media with its mapping capabilities to create a range of effects and possible learning activities. Work with these Google applications was soon connected to work with digital photography and, to a lesser extent, video. By this time in the semester, the teachers and students were just returning from spring break. Mr. Cameron had taken pictures in Ms. Glide's class, and he used them to demonstrate more visual editing tools and how to make digital collages. He also introduced the teachers to additional photo resource sites like Flickr and reviewed with them on how to combine audio and visual texts and how to embed them in podcasts, blogs, and PowerPoint presentations.

Based on where things were at this point in the semester, it was decided to not go too deeply into working with video. Before the break, the focus had been to give the teachers significant hands-on exposure with a variety of digital tools, but by this time it seemed necessary to "reset" the focus to give greater attention in the remaining sessions to solidifying links between what the teachers had learned and their actual use of what they had learned in their instructional practices. Yet there were two additional media that were introduced. One was Comic Life, a downloadable application that allowed users to create simple storyboards (somewhat similar to a comic strip) by combining pictures or drawings and written texts. Voice could also be added. The other digital media that was introduced was Second Life. Second Life is a multi-user virtual environment that both mimics and extends activities and interaction possibilities of the real world through the actions of avatars that "residents" of the Second Life world can create and digitally animate. These last two applications allowed Mr. Cameron to further teach and reinforce the ease and viability of integrating different digital media into other digital platforms.

This summary of the design and sequence of activities during the second semester provides context for a closer look at the teachers' actual experiences of learning about and working with podcasts, blogs, Google applications, digital photography, Comic Life, and Second Life. Rather than initially giving this overview and plan to the teachers, however, Mr. Cameron began his first session by asking them what they were already doing in their classes and what else they hoped to learn in the PD sessions. "I pretty much want to know what uses you are making of technology in your classrooms," he told them. "For example, the pen is a form of technology. I'd like to have as much sync as possible. Can someone start regarding what you are doing in your class?" "In the Hip Hop Journalism class," Ms. Foster responded, "we would like to learn how to do podcasting. I think that would help. I also want to use more PowerPoint and word processing. We have been using a lot of the Gmail functions, and I would like to do more work with Photoshop also." "There has been some work with video for shooting and telling stories," a graduate student chimed in. "Is there anyone in science?" Mr. Cameron asked. "I use the DVD to lecture," Mr. Roy said. "What about online resources?" Mr. Cameron asked. Ms. Church responded, "I think that it makes a big difference in doing research. My classes are starting to do research online. We started last year with Citation Creators. You know that company. But not many kids have done that. I would also like to learn how to use blogs." "Anybody doing robotics? Anyone doing gardening? Are there any alternatives to paper, paper and essays?" Mr. Cameron asked. "Now we have the Ya/Ya program for making furniture art, and there is also airbrushing," said Ms. Foster. At this point, the principal talked about his desire to have students learn how to design video games.

Next, everyone was asked to talk about any problems they saw in teaching with technology. The principal noted, "The robustness of the applications exceeds our students' ability, one. And two, their innovation and excitement exceed the robustness of the applications. So it is the marriage of those two things that I think is sometimes problematic." Mr. Guy noted that a key problem was "consistently functioning technology. . . . If the printer doesn't work, or the computer doesn't work, or not all of the computers are working, its frustrating." Ms. Kim added, "We need a lot of one-on-one attention for the kids to teach technology." "I don't have the greatest and the highest tech skills myself," said Mr. Roy. "Sometimes the challenge is that the teacher doesn't know as much as the kids know, that the kids are ahead of the teacher," a graduate student noted. "But when we are doing projects, the students' attendance gets in the way," added Ms. Church. In response, the principal said, "With some of these applications, if you don't get that very first part, it becomes difficult to do the end product. There is no question that this is going to be a tough challenge." I added, "If everything is working perfectly and these products come out, we don't have from our own training the ability to assess their quality. What is an 'A' youth commentary versus a 'B' commentary, or an 'F' commentary?" Mr. Cameron closed this discussion by showing several interesting examples of young people's work with digital media in Chicago on the iRemix.org website. For the remainder of this session, he guided the participants in creating their first podcasts.

Podcasting

"You know what a 'drop' is in terms of radio?" Mr. Cameron asked. "It is basically when the host says, 'You're listening to WKWE radio; my name is Cameron,' and something like 'I'm going to be your company tonight.'" He told the teachers that for their first podcast, their drop would be their name, the subject they teach, and what they hope to get out of the PD sessions on technology. Everyone's drop was to be no more than 30 seconds, and when they were completed he combined them into a "collective" podcast that was less than four minutes. They also took pictures of themselves using the Mac's Photo Booth application to add to the podcast. Mr. Cameron gave a narration about himself to demonstrate the first drop, then each teacher took a turn. In this way, the teachers were able to quickly see how the application worked.

This initial podcast was played again at the beginning of the next session as a way of reminding the teachers of what they had said as well as how easy it was to create a podcast. At this point, none of the teachers were ready to present anything regarding experimenting with podcasting, and in this session they learned how to do additional things like mixing different kinds of texts in the podcasts and eventually posting them. Mr. Cameron passed out a sheet that listed three steps for producing the podcasts that would be completed during the session: record an interview in GarageBand, mix and edit music with the interview, and publish it. The sheet also had space for the teachers to write out a brief plan for how they might use a podcast with their students. Then he announced,

> When you are starting a podcasting session with your students, I think it is a good idea in the beginning to let them know where it is going to end up. So starting with the end in mind is a good idea because it frames and conceptualizes the activity and what the end product will be. The end product might be in a PowerPoint presentation; the audio might end up on a blog, or it might be burned onto a CD. . . . Do you record on Monday, mix on

Wednesday, and publish it on the web on Friday, so you have a weekly cycle? . . . Knowing your process is the core that you wanna build on.

After the teachers worked on their individual plans, they were asked to work in pairs and use GarageBand to interview each other for one minute, in part to get a sense of how their students might go through the same process. As the teachers worked, they helped each other figure out what they needed to do while Mr. Cameron walked around and answered technical questions like how to add music tracks, how to set the timing for the podcasts, or how to control the sound. The teachers clearly enjoyed "playing" with mixing and posting their podcasts. "This is too much," said Mr. Roy. He was paired with Ms. Kim, who was smiling and obviously pleased as she showed him what she had done. "I really like this," said Mr. Elder from the other side of the computer lab. Ms. Church and Ms. Glide had brought their own laptops so that they could continue to work on the projects at home.

Toward the end of this session, two additional applications that could be used for podcasting were introduced—Audacity and Audio Jack— and their unique features were discussed. The teachers were shown how to download and use both programs. Audacity worked as an audio editing tool in much the same way as GarageBand, while Audio Jack was more powerful in that it could be used to capture any audio signal from any sound source on a computer. Toward the end of this session, Mr. Cameron told the group, "We are not going to have time to go into blogging today, so all we can do is mix down [compress into another digital format] the podcast you worked on and either burn it [on a CD or flashdrive] or send it as an e-mail. Good job ya'll!" Everyone clapped.

Blogging

Learning how to technically use blogs was easy, but developing conceptual frameworks to exploit their affordances was more complex. Mr. Cameron created a PD blog site for collaborative use by the teachers and also helped each teacher create her or his own blog. Over time, the PD blog became a valuable resource in a number of ways. It allowed for a dialogue space for the teachers that ran collaterally to the face-to-face dialogues that were occurring in the sessions and thereby extended dialogue between the teachers in a number of productive ways. The teachers began posting and reading the blog to both inform others and to keep up with what was going on in different classrooms through the continual record that was created. So things were not being posted arbitrarily.

Mr. Guy, for example, had posted a description of his math lesson that used Google Earth to give his students engaging experiences while learning trigonometric functions. He had volunteered to talk about what he had done with this application to the other teachers in line with our PD tradition, and he gave a brief verbal presentation. Teachers had a lot of questions, and he was comprehensive in his answers. Interestingly, a couple of teachers said they did not quite understand what he had done with his class until they read how he had described it on the blog. Ironically, one limitation for Mr. Guy was that he was not able to use math symbols on the blog: "I'd like to find a way to do my notes on the blog, but I can't find a way to do the math script like subscripts, superscripts, and things like that."

Mr. Cameron offered a number of suggestions in the PD sessions for creative ways that teachers could utilize blogs like using them as a platform to publish podcasting projects that were completed in classes, having blogs as a place where they post findings from research projects, or providing topics for students to write about more informally on the blog to offer reluctant writers opportunities for a different form of written expression. He described ways to organize blogs to achieve different goals, noting, "It only gets better with time, because as new students come in, they have the record of everything that you've done and all the perspectives of everybody who came to your class in addition to your knowledge."

More than the actual tool, however, teachers came to see that use of blogs (as well as other digital media) reflected a shift in paradigm that required a concurrent shift in the structures of teaching and learning in classrooms. Blogging was a particularly useful tool for beginning these shifts because it enabled multiple voices, dialogic conversations, and distributed authorship. The PD blog was a key tool that was used to facilitate the development and reflect the contributions of the teachers to the processes of learning in the PD sessions. They posted descriptions of things they were working on and their ideas about what they wanted the sessions to focus on, and they documented some of their plans and goals for what they would do in their classes with the digital tools they were learning to use. These considerations are further discussed later in this chapter in the section "Teaching with Technology."

Google Applications

After working with blogs, the next session was focused on the use of three Google applications: Google Maps, Google Images, and Google Documents. The teachers were guided through using these media to search for pictures, download them, edit them, arrange them in a particular order of compositional design, and finally create a specific Google map and blend the images to make a visual essay or pictorial itinerary that could be used in conjunction with other class activities or assignments. With Google Documents, teachers were shown how they (or their students) could all share the same document, collaboratively edit it, and see the changes taking place in real time.

In the following session, Ms. Glide presented aspects of what she had done with Google Earth in her class. She had her students download, edit, and sequence images that corresponded to the geography of a story that was being read in class and put them into PowerPoint presentations to present the images in sequence. Mr. Cameron had gone to the class to support her work with her students, and he had also taken pictures of the process that, as mentioned earlier, were eventually used to teach about digital photography in a subsequent session. In presenting to the group on this work, Ms. Glide talked about additional things she had learned while working with the application in her classes.

> I did some work with Google Earth this week with the kids, and as usual they were teaching me functions that I did not know existed. Apparently, there is some way to put in place marks like we did with Google Maps, and I am not sure who can do that or how because it's kind of like the same little bubble is gonna pop up. It's something having to do with different layers that you can eliminate or add to that, and I think that would be really interesting. So we are going to work on that some more.

The idea that the presentations could be about work in progress or could present problems that Mr. Cameron, the group, or the principal could help with was an important feature of the professional development, so that teachers could feel comfortable sharing their work with the other teachers and participants in the sessions. Also during this session, I talked about a website that had lesson plans that utilized Google applications for every subject area in high school. Teachers asked to have it posted on the PD website.

Digital Photography

As a part of working with digital photography, Mr. Roy shared things he had been doing in his science class with a gardening project in back of the school. He had his students take pictures of the plants at different stages of growth. He was considering posting the pictures in a blog, but he also sought additional ideas from the group. Mr. Cameron responded, "I think that in the context of the blogs, that's a natural way of maybe documenting it—what's going on with the garden project—just taking pictures from the garden and starting a page and extending that with the information about nutrition awareness, et cetera."

After other teachers made suggestions about additional possibilities for Mr. Roy's project, Mr. Cameron laid out a structure for further working with digital photography in this session. The approach was to have teachers think of a thematic focus related to their discipline and then go online to find at least five pictures that related to that theme or focus. Next, the teachers were to download the pictures, edit them for size and image quality, add some special effects using iPhoto, and then save the pictures in a folder. Mr. Cameron demonstrated the process for the teachers by walking them through the steps on one photo. The last step was to use the photos to create a visual map or essay about the theme. The teachers worked for the rest of the session on this project, which gave them experience in going through several stages and using or developing a number of key skills for doing a range of things with digital photographs.

Comic Life

One entire PD session was spent working with Comic Life. Mr. Cameron felt it was important for the teachers to learn about this tool not only because it was easy to use and fun to play with but also because it could be a powerful way to storyboard plans for a video, documentary, podcast, essay, or any other project that required sequencing ideas. Additionally, he used Comic Life to review and reinforce for teachers the fluid integration possibilities of the different media. "It starts simple," he told everyone in a session toward the end of spring. "I can easily crop these pictures [from Comic Life] and dump them into a podcast, then pair with Ms. Rivers to read all the captions and bounce that to iTunes and into the same podcast. . . . So going from just one storyboard into a podcast, you have two projects with one effort. That's what I mean by the multiple connections of these projects." For the rest of this session, the teachers worked in pairs to experiment with making multiple textual connections while creating an audio/visual or visual/written text story using the digital affordances of Comic Life.

Again, what the teachers experienced, in part, was how fun learning could be both in the process of creating and in the process of sharing. Toward the end of this session, there was discussion about why everyone had enjoyed this process so much and how we could plan for our students to have this kind of feeling about the work they did in classes. This embodying of the actual experiences of learning with digital tools seemed to be one of the most important outcomes of these PD sessions.

Second Life

As noted earlier, Second Life is a virtual world in which "residents" can have social and creative experiences through their control of an avatar that they create. Ms. Glide had agreed to do a unit in two of her English classes using Teen Second Life, and the discussion of her work with students in this unit is the focus of chapter 4. We also wanted the other teachers to have some knowledge of and experience with Second Life, so in May, as the school year moved toward an end, we used a PD session to work with the teachers in Second Life. Mr. Cameron guided the teachers on downloading the program, building individual avatars, and practicing the basic movements and communicative capabilities of the platform. I joined Mr. Cameron in leading this session and also supported Ms. Glide when she did the unit in her class. After exploring a bit "in world" as it is called, we had a lively discussion about possible pedagogical uses and potential problems of this digital media in relation to other media we had worked with during this semester.

Mr. Cameron saw Second Life as another multimodal digital environment that shared some characteristics with media we had already worked with, but he also talked about how it contained key differences. He opened the discussion by saying, "I just wanted to see how people think about this. What are your exposures to this? How do you feel about it? Do you think it's a good thing, a bad thing? What do you think it can help do in a classroom setting?" Ms. Foster raised considerations about privacy, and this led to an extended discussion also about issues of identity, since a person can chose how they want to represent themselves in Second Life through how they create their avatar. We talked about how these issues of identity might affect students both positively and negatively. Mr. Cameron compared Second Life identities to one of the projects in Ms. Foster's class where her students had to create and represent a historical persona or a famous contemporary person; he suggested that creating an avatar just takes this to another plane of the imagination: "That can be in itself an enriching conversation to figure out . . . to really become consciously aware of why people define themselves in a particular way when the options become limitless," he noted.

Clearly, there was not enough time in one session to address all of the considerations for our "first lives" that were raised by a brief experience of Second Life. This will be addressed more fully in chapter 4. But one of the things we were beginning to see in terms of our work in the PD sessions was that we as educators needed to understand how to take better advantage of the kind of learning being enabled by an increasingly widening array of digital media—each with unique capabilities and affordances. We could see that the ways we were learning to teach with technology were only the beginning of what was possible. Such learning was also only the beginning of what was critically needed to effectively transform schools to meet new, complex, and global challenges of life and learning in the twenty-first century.

TEACHING WITH TECHNOLOGY

There were a number of things that all of the V-Tech teachers did over the course of the school year to utilize some aspect of technology in their teaching. One was how each teacher worked to rethink and redesign the physical space and environment of their classrooms. As with the interior design of rooms in a home, what things are present and where things are placed reveals a great deal about the intentions for use and the kinds of activities that will occur in a space. Each of the teachers experimented with developing various kinds of activity centers in their classrooms, and in the second semester, this was augmented by actual designs and implementations of floor plans to more effectively accommodate digital learning, even when there was not extensive use of digital media in a particular classroom. The teachers themselves had experienced working in activity centers at various times in the PD sessions with designated areas for work with different digital tools, and they ultimately saw that the design of the space of the classroom itself was fundamental to enabling other changes in their teaching practices.

Another thing that all of the teachers implemented in their classes and engaged in with each other (although at widely varying levels) was the use of blogs. As earlier noted, the PD blog became a central tool for communication among teachers and other project participants in terms of sharing plans, ideas, and the progress of activities going on in different classrooms. Each teacher also created their own blog as one of the activities in professional development. Once the individual blogs actually existed, all of the teachers found ways to use them in conjunction with instruction at some level. The use of blogs by the teachers was also facilitated by the excitement that some of the students showed in their use of them. This was tied, in part, to the fact that the teachers had some of the same students in their different classes, and they often talked to each other about the work and progress of these shared students.

For example, before one PD session began, Ms. Glide talked with Ms. Foster about the student they each had in their class who did a blog in tribute to his friend that he called his "world wide wall." Ms. Glide told Ms. Foster, "He was so excited about the possibilities and being able to share this with his friends in my class. So whatever you are doing helped him." Ms. Foster then said, "What he is doing in his blog is he created a whole slideshow of a friend of his who was killed. It has 18 pictures in it. So this has been expressed in a way that he is using technology and he is so excited about it." Overhearing this conversation, Mr. Cameron added, "Actually, this morning he was asking me how to add a song to his blog, and I said you have to go to customize, but make sure the song has no profanity. . . . So he goes through the site and pulls up in the blogger feature section a form that gives you the option of putting a warning on the content that you're uploading." Ms. Glide's following response in this conversation was insightful regarding ways the teachers motivated each other (and were motivated by their students) to expand their teaching practices.

Sometimes he wants to stay later. . . . He is so excited. . . . So I thought about blogs, and then I thought, "Well, I have to teach myself more about them." So I found out that all the kids who were in your class were like "Oh yeah, we already have blogs." So now, how to do it well makes my life so much easier because not only do they know how to do it, they know more features than I do. And they can also help a couple of other people who don't know how to do it. So thank you, Ms. Foster.

A few weeks later, Mr. Cameron had observed how Ms. Glide was using blogs in her classes, and commented about it in one of the PD sessions. "As an observer, I have already seen some changes with her students. Just the fact of keeping a blog, and coming here and immediately going towards that, and adding more things or adding portions from assignments, pictures to share with friends. . . . It's having an impact on her students."

These cross-class engagements with students and among teachers also contributed to Ms. Rivers's more extensive use of blogs in her teaching. At first, her use of blogs was more tentative and constricted. She reported to Mr. Cameron that she finally did begin to use her individual blog but that she initially used it "so I don't have to take papers home." By having her students submit assignments on the blog, her work in responding to them had become more portable. Soon she began to notice that a significant change was taking place in the dynamics of her classes as she mediated more work with the blog: "I'm finding that I speak less, and the students do more in class," she noted.

Ms. Rivers also benefited by the fact that other teachers in the school were using blogs in conjunction with the work in their classes, such that a critical mass of student expertise in the use of this digital media was emerging. Since she shared a lot of students with Ms. Foster, Ms. Rivers began letting them extend the use of blogs they had created for Ms. Foster's class to the work that she was assigning in her class. This, of course, required the students to increase the sophistication of their personal blogs by adding partitions for the work of multiple classes and incorporating more digital tools as necessitated by the different assignments. Eventually, Ms. Rivers and Ms. Foster began to collaborate on the assignments they were giving to their shared group of students. They began working together to connect and expand things that were going on in Ms. Foster's journalism class, on the one hand, and Ms. River's social studies classes, on the other, by making assignments that were more comprehensive in the blend of foci and content from both classes.

Ultimately, the work of these two teachers helped us understand that each student needed to have only one academic blog to use for appropriate work and assignments for all of her or his classes at the school.

The role and significance of technology transfers among teachers and students were partially envisioned as an outcome of the professional development, but we did not anticipate the fluidity, serendipity, and, in some cases, sophistication of these transfers. Specifically, we did not fully anticipate the significance of the roles that the students themselves would play in pushing themselves and their teachers to exploit the capabilities of the various media. Another example of this was an episode in which Ms. Church was working with Malik, a student mentioned in chapter 2, as he was trying to add a slideshow to his blog. First, they tried to do it through the iMovie application, but they discovered with the help of Mr. Cameron that a QuickTime file cannot be uploaded into blogger. Malik found another way to do it by using his Gmail account, and was able to make a seamless upload of his pictures. His probing of different media in order to achieve his purpose impressed Mr. Cameron, who noted, "Thinking like designers is where the magic in learning happens, because they bring their own ideas to it."

The teachers as a whole did not make as much use of podcasting as they made of blogging. One exception to this was the work that Ms. Foster did with her students in creating podcasts, discussed in chapter 2. However, most of the teachers experimented with using various Google applications. Earlier in this chapter, I described how Mr. Guy had used Google Earth to help his students learn and practice math functions and, later, how he shared this with other teachers in a PD session. Ms. Glide and Ms. Foster also used Google Maps and other Google Images and had their students incorporate them into PowerPoint presentations. Again, in these activities, it was the students who often pushed the possibilities for what could be done with these media.

Work in Ms. Church's classes also provided interesting examples of ways that teachers were taking what they learned in professional development into their classes. Ms. Church had done a unit that focused on homelessness as a significant issue that warranted more attention in society. She found that the students were more motivated to write essays about these issues when they could add images to their writing or do visual essays. They did Google Image searches for relevant pictures, which added more substance to their work. When the issue in focus switched to HIV/AIDS, the students extended their online work from the incorporation of images to actually doing more research on the Internet at a variety of websites, and they added links to key websites to their final papers. Ms. Church became comfortable with this approach of having the students blending multiple modes of expression into their research projects, and she made plans to continue this approach with them in the next unit that she would be starting, on child soldiers.

Most of the teachers made considerable progress in using more technology in their classes. A couple of the teachers did not do quite as much, but even so, the TEACH Project changed their perspectives on utilizing additional approaches and additional tools, specifically digital tools, to further challenge and engage their students. In some cases, these changes were revealed in things like greater use of the schools' computer labs, even for traditional purposes like writing or typing essays. In other cases, the intense challenges of teaching at a continuation school mitigated things that teachers desired to do in their classes. I was particularly concerned that our project was not able to provide better support to Mr. Roy in his teaching of science classes. Yet, in the final PD session of the school year, he reported that he had joined the Teacher Institute at the Exploratorium, a science museum that has exemplary programs to support the teaching of science. "If you go to this two-year [after-school and summer] teacher program," he told us, "then you have access to their resources forever. . . . So if I know I'm gonna have access to computers and if I'm gonna have other science resources in my classroom, I'll let them know, and they'll help me integrate technology."

4 | "VIRTUAL" WORLD MEDIA

The image shown in figure 3 is from Teen Second Life, the youth version of Second Life. This multi-user virtual environment is free for teens under 18. They can access the features of this MUVE by creating an avatar whose image and actions they control; then they can move around and do things in this world. It was originally established as a site where teens could meet, create things, socialize, and make friends using text chats and even voice communication. For example, they can use their avatars to chat and interact with other avatars, to build an infinite range of objects or structures, and to travel to various places that have been built primarily by other "residents" as well as the Linden Lab hosts of this virtual environment. At any time, they can use a camera option to snap a photograph of their avatar or some other object at a specific location in the world and e-mail it to themselves or to others as a "postcard."

Fig. 3. Teen Second Life

The postcard in figure 3 depicts the avatar of a young man I will call Terrance, a 17-year-old V-Tech student who was in Ms. Glide's World Media class during the second semester of the academic year. Some of the work on digital projects, the interactive communication, and the other class activities of Terrance, a young woman I will call Jada, and a number of students in this class are focused on in this chapter to exemplify the nature of learning and instruction during a two-week curricular unit in Teen Second Life. Terrance named his avatar "GReala Blitz," but he was not entirely satisfied with the way it looked. He noted that he was "still learning how to create him."

GReala Blitz sits on top of a "world" that Terrance created. The avatar is looking down on a structure Terrance built as a multifaceted club or presentation space for performances in spoken word, rap music, and hip-hop dance. The floor of his club is composed of a modified picture of Terrance's face that he took using his computer's Photo Booth application, and the design on the wall behind the stage is a snapshot of the shirt and chain he was wearing. As his skills developed, he was able to integrate various shapes, textures, colors, animations, and sounds into his design. On a number of occasions, he stayed after school to continue working in the computer lab on projects even after the unit in Teen Second Life came to an end.

Terrance's postcard reflects some of the new literacy practices that came into play in Ms. Glide's World Media class during a two-week curricular unit in which her students learned to create, communicate, and explore through the affordances of Teen Second Life. In this chapter, I discuss how these practices complicate our notions of (and the interactions between) texts and experience. I describe how they project new dynamics of mind and body, of "virtual" and "real," of space and place, of production and consumption, and of the hyperconnectivity of different expressive modalities. I argue that they offer emergent ways to both create and constrain meaning and identity, agency and power, and culture and pleasure as these constructs are mediated digitally and transmitted globally. I show how viable examples of project-based learning were realized in individual and joint productive activities that reflected significant forms of academic discourse, inquiry, and accountability among and between the students and their teacher(s). I also address key problems that occurred in attempting to utilize a virtual environment for learning in the real world of Ms. Glide's class.

Unlike Ms. Foster, the highly experienced teacher of the Hip-Hop Journalism class, Ms. Glide was in her first year of teaching during the year the TEACH project was implemented. As noted in the first chapter, she started the year being very tentative about using any technology in her classes. She was particularly concerned that her students might know significantly more about the use of various kinds of digital media than she did. In the previous chapter, I described how she and her teacher colleagues at V-Tech gained greater confidence and competence, albeit unevenly, in trying different ways to incorporate more technology into their instruction. By the second semester, Ms. Glide was regularly using the computer lab for some of her class activities, and by the middle of that semester, she felt that she was ready to do a unit utilizing Teen Second Life in her two World Media classes.

There have been concerns raised about the adult version of Second Life, in which about nine million avatars reportedly interact on a digital landscape, in some cases to achieve real-life purposes like selling products, doing research, conducting classes, and even recruiting for college admissions (Bugeja 2007). There are concerns, for example, about "griefing," where one person's avatar harasses the avatar of another person. Linden Lab, the host of this virtual environment, has worked to mitigate these concerns in the teen version, in part by its age restriction for use of 17 years old and under. This is why V-Tech's principal felt comfortable getting authorization to unblock Teen Second Life to provide access for the school's use.

Ms. Glide was supported in implementing this unit by me and two other students from the university who worked with the TEACH Project. One of these students, Ms. Canon, was a key member of our support team (especially with respect to technical support), because she had worked with an earlier research project called the Fractal Village that took place at V-Tech for three weeks during the middle of the first semester of the school year. As part of a dissertation study for which I was a committee member, its focus was to facilitate eight V-Tech student volunteers in learning about fractals and other mathematical concepts through building things in Teen Second Life. Since the TEACH team had already planned to work with Teen Second Life during the second semester of the school year, I was able to support the Fractal Village Project by letting it use TEC Island, a virtual space for which I purchased a one-year lease from Linden Lab, the company that owns Second Life.

Consequently, a few students in the school had experiences with this virtual environment seven months before the unit in Ms. Glide's class, and two of these students were actually in her class.

The other university student volunteered to work with us on this unit for several of the days that it ran. But most often, there were three adults in the computer lab to guide and support the students' activities—Ms. Glide, Ms. Canon, and me. We met before the intervention to plan these activities, and decided that we wanted to focus more on attempting to understand specific ways that the students' learning developed through their experiences with this particular form of virtual, digital media, rather than only trying to make explicit links to Ms. Glide's established curriculum. In the two-week time frame of the unit, we decided to closely follow the work of building the avatars that were needed to access the MUVE in conjunction with the virtual and real identity work involved. Next, we wanted to encourage and follow students in their building of a variety of digital objects on TEC Island, particularly objects or structures that might incorporate other kinds of media, like photographs, video, voice recordings, or music. Here our focus would be on their continuing development of digital or computational literacy skills as well as on their communication and interactions with others both in the classroom and in the virtual world. We also wanted to encourage their travel to various sites in Teen Second Life to expand their skills, experiences, and perceptions of possibilities in this world.

Data for this unit was collected through direct observation and field notes along with a stationary camera that was used to record activities and conversations connected to the unit that took place in the school's computer lab. The transcriptions of the recordings were used mainly to capture the general discourse in the classroom (the discussions among students and between students and teachers), rather than attempting to capture things on the computer screens with the camera. Selected things that were produced by the students on the computers were captured using the features of Teen Second Life that allowed for snapshots of screens as well as text chats to be saved and turned into documents and artifacts. Students also did quick writes about some of their experiences with this media, and five were interviewed. These data were augmented and triangulated with my descriptive, reflective, and analysis field notes; reflective field notes by Ms. Canon and Ms. Glide; and interviews with Ms. Glide before and after the intervention.

CLASSROOM CONTEXT

Ms. Glide taught two 55-minute periods of World Media that were scheduled during the last two periods of the school day. These were humanities-centered courses that had a focus on global issues like the environment, world poverty, and global and local conflicts, and she used the same curriculum for both periods. Because of the achievement levels of most V-Tech students when they arrive at the school, one central objective of these classes was to strengthen their reading, writing, and analysis skills. Before the unit utilizing Teen Second Life, Ms. Glide had done units that focused specifically on writing development and social science analysis. She had worked extensively with her students on traditional writing genres like exposition and persuasion that were aligned with the California state standards for English–Language Arts. They had worked, for example, on structuring logical arguments, on the use of rhetorical devices to support assertions, on defending positions with relevant evidence, and on ways to appeal to emotions or systems of belief.

In conjunction with their writing of essays, Ms. Glide also had her students write about literary, social, and global issues in blogs. This allowed them to incorporate a variety of multimedia texts as well as draw on Internet sources to further support or develop ideas that they initially presented in their essays. Essentially, she wanted her students to first get the traditional approach to writing, then explore various technologies to see how their use might deepen understandings of techniques of written persuasion. In addition to creating and writing their own blogs, students also read and wrote responses to other blogs that were addressing topics that were being focused on in the class. In extending traditional classroom activities to incorporate elements of digital media, she was attempting to facilitate her students' writing development through the features of a wider range of textual mediums. So her work with this class was often split between the classroom and the computer lab, and in both sites, she guided students to work both individually and collaboratively. She noted,

> Given the flexibility that the course allows, I employ a variety of teaching methods and a range of activities to meet these broad objectives. For example, students conduct Internet research, critique films, and analyze and respond to literature. Units are created around themes such as "Conflict and Resolution" and contain a variety of assignments that allow students to demonstrate their knowledge in different ways.

Most of the students in the World Media classes were sophomores and juniors, although this delineation was problematic given the actual credits earned by individual students. The total enrollment for both classes was 44 students (22 in each class), of which 18 were males and 26 were females; 33 were African American, 8 were Latino, 2 were Asian/Pacific Islander, and 1 was White. As noted in the first chapter, however, Ms. Glide found that there were rarely more than 15 students in attendance in each class on any given day, and that was one of the biggest obstacles to their achievement. Additionally, of her 44 students enrolled in these two classes, 10 had Individual Education Plans (IEPs) required for students with designated learning disabilities. Although most students revealed key problems in their abilities to write and read, overall skill levels still varied tremendously. Despite these obstacles, Ms. Glide assessed that her students had many strengths and enjoyed working on things that connected to their interests, particularly when computers were employed, even though she saw that they could also become distracted during their work with computers.

In some K–12 educational settings, the forms of technology like those Ms. Glide had begun to use—computers for writing and Internet searches, creating and responding to blogs and class websites, the use of whiteboard and PowerPoint presentations—have already been incorporated into instruction. Most often, the use of these technologies is directly linked to traditional structures for teaching and learning that can also be employed to a significant extent without the use of digital tools. This is what was described earlier in Ms. Glide's use of blogs to connect to the genre-based writing that her students were assigned as an integral part of her curriculum.

However, technologies like Teen Second Life, video games, and other new media that offer interactive experiences in virtual worlds have, for the most part, not found a place in the life and learning of schools. One discipline that is somewhat of an exception to this point is science, where significant work is being done with 3-D modeling tools to model various scientific phenomena in order to help students develop conceptually richer understandings beyond the limits of traditional textbooks, lectures, and discussions. An important aspect of computational modeling that is just as significant for cognitive development in other disciplines as it is in science is that it allows students to visualize abstract concepts by creating structures through which they can explore and experiment. Importantly, these rich understandings are distributed across all phases of the modeling process, including the learning about and use of the computational tools needed to construct the models. This approach to learning in a virtual environment through building things that model or go beyond physical reality is a central aspect of the activities in Teen Second Life. Yet for most educators, there is still resistance to using new media and virtual world technologies that can model or expand physical reality, and this resistance is not entirely an expression of technophobia. For example, as Berry (2008) noted, "The newest virtual environments threaten traditional classrooms—challenge hierarchies, wrench authority away from teachers, distribute rather than individuate knowledge and disrupt traditional forms of assessment."

Essentially, the use of certain forms of new media necessitates dramatically different approaches to teaching and learning, and the TEACH Project's work with Teen Second Life in Ms. Glide's class was, in part, an attempt to explore these differences. Rather than linking her students' work in this world directly to her established curriculum, we were interested in understanding more of the specific nature of their learning and literacy development as it was revealed in their constructing of identities; their travel to different sites in the world; their building of various digital objects; and their communication, interactions, and collaborations with peers and others as they experienced and explored this virtual world. Ms. Glide introduced the unit to her students by saying, "We've been talking about world media and trying to understand what's going on in different worlds, and Second Life is another kind of different world."

CONSTRUCTING IDENTITIES

Virtual, three-dimensional learning environments can be leveraged to create opportunities for students of all ages to learn about an array of topics (math, art, music, science, literature, geography, astronomy, etc.) in completely new ways (Barab et al. 2000). For example, the earlier Fractal Village Project worked with eight V-Tech student volunteers in Teen Second Life to support the development of computational literacy and mathematical reasoning. A key thing that the Fractal Village Project attempted to foster was the development of the students' mathematical identities through their virtual activities, to see if that could transform their real mathematical identities.

In Ms. Glide's class, we also saw that acts of identity construction were central to the kinds of learning that took place in Teen Second Life, and we found that the students' processes of developing particular personal identities in the virtual world were decidedly different from traditional notions of intellectual identity. Noddings (2006) linked the development of academic rigor and critical thinking in high school disciplines to processes for self-understanding that connected broader aspects of students' lives to their explorations of challenging issues. This connection of the academic and the personal was a key strategy for Ms. Glide's earlier work in the class, but we wanted to see how it might be uniquely revealed in the Teen Second Life unit as her students constructed personal, virtual identities that could link to their developing identities as learners.

Constructing an "in-world" identity by creating an avatar that was needed to access the features of the site was one of the students' first digital learning experiences. For example, Terrance, who was mentioned at the beginning of this chapter, was not happy with the look of his avatar, in part because he was "still learning how to create him." His statement reflects two aspects of the learning that began immediately in this site while constructing an in-world identity with an avatar—not only the computational literacy skills that were required, but also the cultural context and constraints that were realized while creating, communicating, interacting, and moving in this virtual world.

Computational literacy skills that were developed and/or reinforced began with getting to the site online; going through a rather complicated registration process, which included selecting a name for one's avatar and providing a telephone number or e-mail address; retrieving log-in confirmation codes via subsequent e-mails or text messages from Linden Lab, which took about 20 minutes; and using the selected name and code that was received to log into the virtual world. Ms. Glide had given her students an assignment sheet that listed these steps, which we wanted them to go through on the first day of the unit to get started with the project. She told them that they would get credit for completing each stage of the project, beginning with getting logged in and creating an avatar. Although these may seem like mundane activities, the students were experiencing how the site worked through multiple digital texts and interfaces—the Internet, cell phone texts, and e-mails. Loud cheers could be heard intermittently in the class as each student successfully completed the process of getting logged in. Some called their friends over to their computer as if to get verification that they were in. "I just got in as 'BigO Footman,'" one student exclaimed. "I got 'Doe Magic,'" his friend responded. (I use the student avatar names in this chapter because these selected names and TEC Island itself are no longer being used and no longer exist in this MUVE.)

As noted earlier, Teen Second Life's basic approach to building understanding and proficiency with specific computational literacy skills was through model building. Essentially, the process of building the avatar modeled the building of all objects and structures in the world, no matter how complex they became. So the activities for constructing identity apprenticed the learning and skills that the students needed to develop for every aspect of building in the site. Researchers like Pea (1993) and Salomon (1993) argued that the understanding of any concept, process, or practice was attributed to and distributed across the physical, temporal, and spatial occurrences through which the competencies had emerged. In other words, according to Lave (1988), cognition is "stretched over, not divided among mind, body, activity, and culturally organized settings which include other actors" (1), and resources from each of these domains were critical to the processes through which competent actions emerged.

In our first class in Teen Second Life, Ms. Canon, one of the university students who had helped with the earlier Fractal Village Project, gave a brief demonstration of some of the tools used for building an avatar by using an LCD projector to project the images on her computer onto a large screen in the lab. These tools allow one to design, shape, and color the features and clothing of a range of stock male or female avatars in order to customize their appearance within a wide range of options. For example, in the adult version of the game, a resident can get over 100,000 items of avatar clothing and accessories for free. Ms. Canon also used the site's "camera view" tool to show her avatar at different angles and doing different things, like walking, running, sitting, gesturing, and dancing. When students were able to log in, they would first go to Orientation Island to begin creating their avatars. Eventually, they would learn how to make their avatars fly as well as how to teleport them directly to other locations in this world.

Ms. Glide began the first computer lab class in Teen Second Life by reminding her students to select a last name for their avatar from the assignment sheet she had given them and then to make up a first name to go with it. "Making your avatar is the main thing we want to get done today," she announced. The assignment sheet had a list of the most recent last names that the virtual world provided, and all residents have to select from these lists for a last name. However, new residents are allowed to create their own first name. The names on the list seem to be constructed such as to not reflect any specific cultural content. So they rarely used actual words, although there were a few on Ms. Glide's list, like "Footman," "Haystack," "Magic," and "Twine." Most were made-up words like "Ansar," "Clowes," "Parx," and "Fhang." The list that Teen Second Life provides is changed frequently.

Most students were quite unhappy with the last names that the site offered for their selection. "I don't like these names," one female student said immediately in a tone loud enough for everyone in the room to hear. "Nobody does," another student responded just as vociferously. They were reacting to what they perceived as an unwelcoming context for ways they would be comfortable representing themselves with respect to a fundamental and important aspect of identity—a person's name. Although Teen Second Life attempted to provide last names that were not culturally specific, Ms. Glide's students felt constrained by having to associate themselves with these kinds of names. Instead of seeing the names as somewhat culturally neutral, they interpreted them as names for white people or as foreign names that were difficult for them to identify with or feel good about using for their avatars.

This problem was partially mitigated by the students' ability to choose first names that they marked with cultural content. For example, Doe Magic used a word that communicated specific cultural content, as in "Do you feel me, doe?" Real Twine was connecting to the significance of being "real" in black culture. A number of girls chose the last name "Fhang," adding first names like "Precious" or "Fa." One girl selected "Fhang" because she felt it had "an Asia background." She was not Asian, but she noted that she wanted to create an avatar that looked like "an Asian American beautiful woman." BigO Footman said, "I chose this name because it was the first name that popped in my head, and it's funny to me." Another student turned the joke on the MUVE and also caused a big discussion in the class by slipping through the name "Osamabinladen Raviprakash" for his avatar. When the student sitting next to him asked Terrance why he chose the first name "GReala," he explained that the G stood for "Gangster." So, beyond the sound correspondence with "gorilla," the name he had given his avatar was meant to signify "a real gangster."

At times, the students' disaffection with the last names required by Teen Second Life had unintended consequences, like they would forget their last names (or forget how to spell them, since they were unusual) and then find that they could not log in and get online unless they called Linden Lab. At the beginning of one class, Ms. Glide told a student who didn't remember his avatar's name and password that he would have to call in to reset them in order to get started that day. Misunderstanding the overlapping identities at the intersections of real and virtual worlds, he said a bit defiantly, "I'm not calling no avatar." Getting through the initial registration and log-in process was a struggle for a number of students at the beginning of the unit. Interestingly, two V-Tech students who had worked on the Fractal Village Project helped us get everyone registered. Jada was one of these students, and she was also a student in the World Media class. She named her avatar "Sweetie Mayako." The other young man just dropped by the class at the beginning to help out. Ms. Glide noted, "For some students who were frustrated with the sign-up process, it really diffused the negative energy to have peers helping them."

Ms. Canon, our resident expert, sometimes showed frustration with the MUVE herself. "Our students were limited by Second Life itself," she reflected. "The log-in process is definitely not friendly to our students, and the default avatars aren't made to represent minority races very well. Second Life is really geared toward the white middle class." She noted that these problems had also frustrated the students in the Fractal Village Project, yet because of that she was more prepared to deal with the technical and cultural issues that came up in Teen Second Life. For example, as she was modeling how to build an avatar, the site was running very slowly at the time, but she was still able to talk the students through the basic things they needed to do. Yet she did not always conceal her feelings, as indicated in her following instructions: "So when you guys go through the registration process, you pick up a default avatar, which is kind of boring, but you get to redevelop the avatar to make it more customized."

Despite the constraints, the students' work to customize their avatars revealed ways that constructing these virtual identities connected to their real identities and to their learning. They talked excitedly to peers and to the adults in the class about how they wanted their avatars to look. Ms. Glide noted, "The girls spent far more time on the appearance of their avatars (face, body, and clothing), while almost all of the boys made comments about being dissatisfied with the clothing, hair, and shoe options." Students wanted to make interesting-looking avatars, but they often ended up spending a lot of time trying to remove or change objectionable aspects of the available clothing and of the default avatars. For example, several of the students wanted to make the skin tone darker, but they were dissatisfied because of the inability to make the tools of the virtual environment do so to their liking. Others, however, made avatars that didn't attempt to mirror their actual appearance.

As with the students in Ms. Foster's Hip-Hop Journalism class, the young men in Ms. Glide's class wore baggy jeans, loose-fitting hooded sweatshirts, and athletic shoes. The male clothing options in Teen Second Life were usually tight-fitting shirts and pants and odd-looking shoes. Most of the young men just wanted their avatar to have clothing that looked like what they actually might wear. They complained about the hair not looking right. One student tried to give his avatar a "fade," a black haircut style. They also complained about the eyelashes being too long and about the shirts being too short and tight. Ms. Glide commented that her male students were concerned about not wanting their avatars to "look gay." Despite these obstacles, she noted, "Almost all of the students were immediately engaged in designing their avatars. Several of the girls and some of the boys who have really struggled with attendance, assignments, and focus were unusually engaged, self-disciplined, and self-directed, which was a noticeable change."

During the first two days of the unit, the students worked hard on building their avatars, changing the styles and colors of their clothing and hair, and eventually teleporting to other places to explore and experience other things in the virtual world. We could see how productive most of the students' experiences were as they worked on their avatars. A student who named her avatar Saysay Snoodie, for example, was really excited about giving it short, bright-colored hair, even though she had long black hair. She had an extended discussion with Ms. Canon about her choices and how to implement them as she experimented with the digital tools to construct her design. "I like the punk rock, funky look," the student said. "I wanted to make her look very unique, but normal looking at the same time." Jada had a similar objective for her avatar and commented, "She's beautiful, but hella thick than me. I swear she is. I don't know why she's like that." Another student who had often been disaffected was absorbed in making his "Osamabinladen" avatar. He wanted it to look like Osama Bin Laden, but Ms. Canon teased him by saying it really looked like Jesus. Yet he managed to get it to where he was satisfied with the look. When asked why he chose to make this avatar, he joked,

"Because I'm a terrorist." Ms. Glide noted that this student, whose attendance had been sporadic all semester, came just about every day during this unit.

One thing that we all noticed was the quality of conversations going on in the classroom among the students and between students and adults. Though the conversations were often quite animated at the various computer stations, they were also mainly focused on work that was being done. Each station had two desktop computers, and students were constantly turning their screens to each other to show what they were doing or calling others over to see something they had created or to get help with a problem. They sometimes gathered to look over each other's shoulders, or they knelt down beside each other as they worked and also shared what they were doing. For example, when one student finished building his avatar, "Real Twine," he called a couple of other students over to look at how it turned out. His pride in the avatar he created was also a reflection of how he had developed his skill with the digital tools. Earlier, he was clearly not comfortable with his avatar and told a friend, "He look the way he is now because I just started. But give me time, I'm gonna make my second person nice." When he finished he said, "I gave him a look that makes him stand out from everybody else." He was happy to find out that he could take a snapshot of his completed avatar and send it to himself as a keepsake via e-mail.

Two students who both had dreads themselves were set on their avatars having dreads. "How can I give my avatar dreads," one of them called out to no one in particular. He had named his avatar "Ripcarl Magic." "Then he's gonna be hatted up," he continued. This student later reported that he wanted his avatar to "look like me 'cause I wear black all the time, and I put my dreads in a ponytail." This was a student who earlier had vocally complained about having to do this project. "What am I going to get out of this. I don't want to do this," he said at first. Before long, however, he was working hard on his avatar. At one point, he showed it to the student next to him, who looked over and said, "You still got a bald spot." Another student came over to help, but they were not able to figure out how to attach dreads to the avatar.

It turns out that the only way to get dreads was to buy them. They were not in the regular Teen Second Life "inventories." Ripcarl Magic asked, "How do I get money?" We had Linden dollars, the currency of Second Life. The site has its own foreign exchange called Lindex, and in the real world, Linden dollars can be traded against U.S. dollars at the rate of one dollar to 270 Linden dollars. But adults cannot give this in-world money to teens, even when they are authorized, as Ms. Canon was, to have an avatar in Teen Second Life for educational purposes. This problem was eventually solved, and some students were able to purchase things like dreads, stylish clothing, or even a cell phone to dress up the look of their avatars. But there were a lot of free things too, and as they found items to augment the look of their avatars, the young women would sometimes offer compliments to each other like "Look at yourself! You look fresh with those shades on." When GReala Blitz received some Linden dollars, he said, "I'm rich." "How are you rich?" Real Twine asked. "I'm rich in my second life," he responded.

Ripcarl Magic, who started out vocally resisting the project, ended up deciding to download the Teen Second Life program on a computer at home to continue exploring it. He reported, however, that it operated very slowly on his home computer, and therefore he did not really play the game there. But he came to class eager to play. At this point in the project, through extensive play with alternative identities, the students were also experimenting with new identities as digital learners. Even in these early stages in the unit, the students were engaging in experiences that reflected some of the principles of learning that the TEACH Project focused on like multimodal learning in semiotic domains where students' meaning-making activities were being stretched across multiple sign systems that included images, words, sounds, symbols, and other kinds of artifacts. In building avatars, they had to attend to the actions, gestures, movements, communication, and some metalevel thinking about the play of semiotic domains across the borders of real and virtual worlds. These kinds of earlier experiences positioned them more as active, collaborative, and even critical learners as they worked to understand as well as to question the experiential frameworks they were receiving through this digital media. I will also show examples of their enacting the probing principle that has been discussed earlier in this book as these students traveled around and explored in this virtual world.

Importantly, as they were learning to take on, make choices about, and play with identities that were virtually new and sometimes problematic, they were also expanding their fundamental sense of identity through learning experiences that were overtly predicated on identity work and connections. Gee (2004) outlined "a tripartite play of identities as learners relate, and reflect on first their multiple real-world identities, then their virtual identity, and finally a projective identity" (208). In other words, the real identity of the person expands to include the virtual identity of the character or role that the person takes on in the 3-D media, and this relationship is enacted through the projective identity, which is the kind of character that the person wants to be in the virtual world.

During the unit, Ms. Glide's students became aware of and enacted these overlapping identities at various levels and in interesting ways. For example, the student who made the statement "I'm not calling no avatar" recognized a distinction between his real identity and that of an avatar but mistakenly assumed that Ms. Glide was asking him to communicate with his avatar as if it had an embodied identity of its own. Some students tried to closely link their real and virtual identities by making the avatars look exactly like them. Ripcarl Magic, for example, dressed his avatar entirely in black because, as he said, "I wear black all the time." Others, like Real Twine, established greater distinction between a real self and "my second person." Jada's comment about her avatar "She's . . . hella thick than me. . . . I don't know why she's like that" revealed a sense of the connection between her real and virtual identities in a way that attributed a kind of agency to the virtual that might be connected to how she was also projecting identity. Jada was slender, but her avatar was "thick," and her comment "I don't know why she's like that" implied that the avatar had a kind of life of her own despite having been created by Jada.

So, Doe Magic, BigO Footman, Real Twine, Ripcarl Magic, Fa Fhang, Saysay Snoodie, Sweetie Mayako, GReala Blitz, and the other avatars were not disembodied illusions but interconnected, multilayered characters used to experience virtual living and learning in a real world. These virtual, representational selves were not throwaway identities of real selves; instead, their construction and activities extended the play and complexity of enacting and interacting identities. In so doing, they changed the context of (and perhaps some constraints on) the emergence of new perceptions and ideas about the world and about being in the world. One consideration is that the representational self of the avatar and the actual self of the person are connected by a mediational self that is distinct in its role as the nexus of interaction and control. With this perspective, we were able to observe the mediational selves of Ms. Glide's students positioned in front of the computers while animating their avatars' travels to real places in the virtual world.

WORLD TRAVELING

"Are these real people?" a student said out loud when his avatar encountered other avatars after he first teleported to one of the active locations in Teen Second Life. As the unit progressed, students continued to experiment with the appearance of their avatars, but they were anxious to get to some of the other sites in the world. For example, as he came into class on the third day of the unit, Ripcarl Magic said, "I'm tired of just walking around in Second Life. Can I do something else?" We had already planned to show the students how to teleport to other sites and to let them explore, and after we showed them how to teleport, Ripcarl Magic and the other students were content to travel around the virtual world for the rest of the period. He eventually found a music site called Def Jay that was a kind of nightclub, and he seemed to enjoy figuring out how to play the music at the site while he looked at artwork and other artifacts there.

Ripcarl Magic had stumbled on a model for what we had planned as the main project for the unit. We wanted the students to design and build a studio, gallery, or loft to use as a multipurpose interactive presentation space in which they could incorporate other digital projects that they could do or had already done like podcasts, photography, video clips, or music tracks. It could also be used to host performances of music, dance, rap, spoken words, and so on.

The more Ripcarl Magic explored this and other sites, the more he got into experiencing and learning about this world. Eventually, he called me over and said, "Excuse me. How do you say something?" I showed him how to text and chat, and he was off again on his journey. The other students were also enjoying visits to various sites, but even after the class ended, Ripcarl Magic stayed and continued to explore. "Can you talk on this?" he asked Ms. Canon. "Yeah, but you don't have a microphone that you need," she replied. All of the students had left the computer lab, and the adults had begun an informal meeting to assess how things had gone and to work on our skills for building objects in preparation for the next phase of the unit. All the while, we could hear Ripcarl Magic talking out loud to no one in particular as he also chatted online with a female avatar he had met. Suddenly he said, "Hey, she just kissed me." He turned from his screen and realized that the only other people in the lab were the three adults. "That girl was following me," he told us, although we hadn't asked anything. "Where'd everybody go?" he asked finally. "I guess I'm 'bout to leave. How do I get out"? Ms. Glide showed him how to log off.

Ripcarl Magic had become more absorbed in his second life than most students in the class. But the other students were also experimenting with travel and online, real-time chats along with other virtual experiences. Our thought was to get them to all offer friendship to each other and thereby be able to track and join other classmates at anytime while in the virtual environment. This goal never quite came to fruition during the unit. However, we did follow and get accountings of many of their experiences as they traveled. We taught them how to teleport to different locations. Some initially experienced frustration with travel because they had trouble getting either into or out of places. One student who was stuck in a location said not so jokingly, "Beam me up, Scottie!"

Generally, the students were good about helping each other find different places and things and about trying to answer each other's questions. They talked to other avatars that were online and learned how to get free stuff to wear or to place in their inventories for future use. They also talked to other avatars to find out about cool places to go. For example, when Ms. Glide asked one student how he got to a particular site, he responded, "I don't know. Someone I met walking around gave me the coordinates."

Their travels and interactions helped them become aware of a wide range of self-representations and alternative ways of being in the world. One student, for example, told the person at the computer next to her, "I was talking to someone, and he was just sitting on a couch talking to me, and he had a big Jesus pin on." Another student asked no one in particular, "Do they know who I am? Do they know that I'm at school or something?" He was talking to someone in the world and commenting out loud about the different things going on in the interaction. "Ah, they laughing at me," he said. A little later, he said, "Um, he just broke on me. These are white people. He told me his name was Brett." They also encountered avatars with green skin and purple hair, ones that were gigantic or diminutive, and others that looked like animals or robots. It surprised some of Ms. Glide's students that these were avatars of people who could be anywhere on earth. Sometimes, they needed to use the MUVE's map feature to get around, or they needed to get orientations on how to use certain things—things that other residents had made and left available for everyone's use, like cars, helicopters, and even guns.

Several male and a couple female students were definitely interested in getting guns for their avatars and learning how to fire them. Ms. Canon said that she thought some avatars had come to TEC Island and left a stash of guns. When Doe Magic got a gun, he jokingly asked her, "Can I get arrested in Second Life?" "You can get in trouble for hacking, but that's about all," she answered. "Can you shoot people?" he continued. "Yes!" Jada answered. "How do you shoot a gun?" he continued "Do you know how to shoot a gun?" Jada knew how to put guns into her inventory that she could then attach to her avatar and carry around, but she did not know how to shoot them. We didn't teach them how to shoot guns, but we understood their fascination with this feature of the virtual environment from their play with video games. We also realized that even though it has a more open-ended script, Second Life was also a game, and residents often called themselves players. This unit in the World Media classes was influenced, in part, by scholars like Gee (2004) and Shaffer (2006) who have conceptualized ways that video games and computer games facilitated types of learning and literacy development.

Although our intent was not to look at traditional video games like those the students might already be playing, there were a couple of times during the unit when the video game possibilities of Teen Second Life inadvertently erupted in the class. For example, at one point during the part of the unit in which we were encouraging students to travel and explore, Terrance, whose avatar was GReala Blitz, yelled out excitedly to the class, "Hey look. They fightin' man. Look. They fightin'." Jada and a couple other students went over to his computer station. "Hey," he said, "you want me to tell you what they said?" He laughed loudly. Jada said, "I want to go where you are. You better get up out of there before they shoot you. I think he's really shooting at you." The sound of gunfire could be heard. A student calls out from the other side of the lab, "Y'all playin' Grand Theft Auto?" From where I was standing, I could see several avatars hiding behind or inside of different structures at the site and firing rifles at each other. Eventually, one of them started shooting in the direction of Terrance's avatar. Terrance made GReala Blitz run in the opposite direction, and the other avatar gave chase while still shooting. GReala Blitz ran around a corner and down a narrow street, then hid inside of one of the buildings. The students who had gathered around Terrance's computer where shouting out suggestions for what he should do next. The hostile avatar walked around the corner, paused for a moment, and peered down the long street. Then it turned around and went back toward the battle with the other armed avatars. Before returning to their computers, the young men talked excitedly for a while about how to make Teen Second Life work like a video game.

We had suggested particular sites that the students should visit, but in the travel stage of the unit we also wanted them to follow their intuitions and discover things. So we tried to exercise restraint rather than being overly directing about where the students traveled. Students found a number of interesting sites that had been designed by residents that showcased various affordances of the MUVE. They saw beautiful landscapes with dramatic mountain backdrops and animated by waterfalls and trees swaying in the wind; urban scenes with drivable cars, motorcycles, trains, planes, and helicopters; and colorful structures that had unusual shapes and textures and purposes. They met characters along the way that ranged from interesting to odd. Our key purpose for the students' travel in the world was for them to develop their skills in manipulating the virtual environment in order to enhance their experiences, through learning how to move, gesture, chat, and text; how to interact with other avatars, including ones that were unfamiliar; how to find places and things using maps, coordinates, and teleporting; how to attach objects to their avatars or put them in inventories for future use; and how to do things like drive or fly. As they traveled, we also knew they would see many interesting and unusual things in the vast array of structures and objects that other residents had created, and we felt this would seed their imaginations for things they could also learn to design and build.

CONSTRUCTING OBJECTS

After focusing on creating avatars during the first two days and on traveling in the world during the next two, we worked with students on building things on TEC Island for the remainder of the two-week unit. Ms. Canon was not available on the last day of the first week in the unit, and this was the day that we shifted the focus to the students working on projects that required them to build a structure in which additional media could be incorporated, like a house or some kind of interactive presentation or display space. Ms. Glide, Ms. Canon, and I were confident that Jada, one of the V-Tech students from the Fractal Village Project, would be able to begin helping the students get started with this project. I even heard

Ms. Canon ask Jada a technical question about teleporting to get around in Teen Second Life. In addition to working on her own project for the unit, Jada had already helped tremendously in getting the students registered on the website and generally being an additional technical resource to her classmates. Unfortunately, some students in the earlier class were not able to log in due to system maintenance being performed by the MUVE. Even on the computer that Jada was using to project her demonstration, the Teen Second Life program was moving much slower than normal. Nevertheless, for the first 20 minutes at the beginning of each class, 16-year-old Jada competently led her peers in developing some of the fundamental skills needed for constructing objects.

Ms. Glide introduced Jada by saying, "Right now, Jada is going to show us how to build things. I understand that it is frustrating for some of you who cannot get logged on, but at least you will know how to build when we get all of the kinks worked out. Jada, the floor is yours." Jada sat at the front of the computer lab and used the LCD projector to project her computer's images onto the large screen, like she had seen Ms. Canon do in her demonstrations. I have provided a significant portion of what Jada said while leading the class. She had prepared a lot, and it took a lot for her to get up in front of her peers and lead the class. She started by saying,

> You all got to look, 'cause I'm not going to go back through everything step by step. So you all have to watch what I do. OK, I'm going to go from the beginning. First you go down to the little box that says "build" and click on it, and that gives you all the shapes [called "prims"] that you need in order to build things. I'm about to make a little club or something, so watch how I do it. Are you all paying attention? If not, you're not going to learn.
>
> See how it's a little box over here [called the "sandbox"]. See this little block where the arrow at. If you click somewhere on this box, you can stretch it. If you want to make it like a place you can go in, you can go to "high/low," and it's cutting a path on the inside so that you can get in.
>
> Then I'm going to my inventory, so you can put some textures on it. They have textures that you can put on there, and if you want to make it look like a house, you can make it into a house.
>
> There's this thing over here that lets you rotate an object, move it down or from side to side. Click rotate and that will turn it all around. Click this and it will make it bigger. Click texture and it's the same as when you are making clothes and stuff for your avatar. Like if you wanted to make a silk

shirt, you can click on that if you have it in your inventory. The same goes for textures for your house.

When you see boxes that say "open it," then open it, 'cause they have all kinds of free stuff in them that you can take and put into your inventory and then add it to your house. If you go to Orientation Island, you can get hecka free stuff.

Jada guided the students through building most of the structure of a house and demonstrated how to make walls, windows, doors, stairs, and so on and give them the shapes, textures, and colors that were desired. She seemed to model her presentation on some of the ways that she had learned to work with digital media from her experiences with the earlier Fractal Village Project. This was mixed with a bit of what she might have imagined the role of a teacher should be, in terms of being highly directive. One thing that was not immediately visible in her presentation was the amount of preparation she did. She earlier had built a new house and put it in her inventory in order to be able to show the complete product while explaining how she made each component. She knew that she would not be able to build the entire house from the ground up in the midst of demonstrating each discrete tool. So she had an overall strategy for her presentation that was nicely thought out and reflected her own understanding of how her classmates could learn best by providing alternate insights into the structure of the whole and its constitutive parts and by building on knowledge that they already had from creating clothing for their avatars and linking that prior knowledge and experience to building new objects. But because of the problems with Teen Second Life, she was not able to get to that last stage of her presentation. What she did do, however, revealed a complete grasp of the technical skills needed even though it was not always communicated in the available technical language. For example, she said, "There's this thing over here that lets you rotate an object," yet she also used a number of appropriate technical words like *inventory, animate, rotational, acoustic, texture,* and *gesture.* When students learn vocabulary in relevant contexts, they have better retention of its meaning and more control over its use.

Students in the first class tried to follow her demonstration, but something was lost for those who could not get online. This may be why Jada at one point exhorted them to pay attention. Not long after she finished, however, Teen Second Life started working properly, and more of the students were able to get on. By the time this class was ready to end, several students asked Ms. Glide if they could stay for the second class and continue to work. She said they could if they got permission from their next-period teachers. Two students returned with permission, and several others who were not in Ms. Glide's class also came and asked if they could work with Second Life. Jada gave a similar demonstration in the later class, and with the MUVE operating properly, the students were very focused and able to get more practice with the basic skills of building. After both demonstrations, Jada, Ms. Glide, and I circulated around the lab and worked with individual students as they practiced constructing things.

As we did this during the second class for that day, it became clear that some students still did not know how to teleport to places where they could get free things to incorporate into their projects, so Jada went back to the computer with the projector and got the class's attention again for a brief brushup on this feature. "To teleport," she told them, "you first go to map, and at first you can go to Help Island, or Orientation Island, or there is something you can click on that will show you a list of all the popular places in Second Life. Basically, if you want to go somewhere you can type it in here and click on teleport. You can also search for places. Orientation Island is one place that is like a free world, and you can go there and get some clean stuff."

I use the term *peer pedagogy* to characterize ways that students were able to work with and learn from each other while using digital tools. Jada was out front in the preceding example, but throughout the unit, students both mentored and supported each other's learning in a variety of ways. One of the central ways (partially reflected in the stance that Jada took toward her classmates' learning from her presentation) was what Gee (2004) called "performance before competence" where the learning takes place by doing rather than learning first and doing later—the development of competence by immediately engaging in the desired practices. So, beyond the support provided by the TEACH team, the pedagogical role of Ms. Glide in this unit was dramatically different than it was with her students prior to the unit. As noted in chapter 2 with Ms. Foster's class, the mediation of "material intelligence" was designed into the digital tools. But with 3-D virtual environments, something more seems to have occurred. The analog space of the classroom was reprogrammed into multiple, virtual places that were inhabited subjectively and collectively within myriad, modularly linked, overlapping digital realities.

After the weekend, students came back to the class very excited about designing and building structures on TEC Island. Like Ripcarl Magic did earlier, another student talked about how he had done some things in Teen Second Life at home over the weekend. Ms. Canon was back, and the class began with her giving another demonstration on how to build things. Using the projector with her computer, she built on what Jada had covered by showing students how to operate and incorporate things using different video and audio tools. Using objects that she had created, she also showed them how to animate and add unique textures to objects they might want to make. She asked for someone to build a sign for our TEC Island site, and two students volunteered and started working on that. Soon, almost everyone was working intently on building things, and they all seemed highly engaged. Ms. Glide was amazed by a student that had not been present for the entire first week. She reflected on how, during this single class, "he quickly signed up, designed his avatar, figured out how to teleport, and immediately began trying to build on TEC Island. He stayed through the next period, helping another student while continuing to build his structure. He even stayed after school and, by the time he left, had built an unusual, cylindrical-shaped structure. He was very proud of himself and talked about really enjoying Second Life."

In the second week, in addition to building things, students experimented more with getting and using some of the free stuff that had been made by others. They put their avatars in cars, boats, and planes that were available at various sites and clicked "ride" to drive and play with these vehicles. Spontaneous talk would erupt, such as "I'm going to see what happens if I crash my car"; "Hey, I just stole a helicopter. Can I take it back to my inventory?"; and "I'm at this house, and I hear music." But the students also worked on building their projects, and as Ms. Glide, Ms. Canon, and I walked around the room and helped out, some were attempting to make more complex constructions like houses with automatic sliding doors or animated waterfalls. "Somebody help me. Somebody help me. Somebody help me," one student kept saying until Ms. Glide came over to help him. Essentially, this help took the form of instructional conversations. Sometimes students had to learn how to write the scripts needed to program certain kinds of animations. Most students were proud of what they were building. Wanting others to see what they had done, they said things like "Come check this out, man. This looks good!"

By the end of the two-week unit, Ms. Glide was pleased to see that most of her students had completed making a digital project that was in line with the general goals of the unit. As they completed their projects, students would often call Ms. Glide over to show off their work. "Come look," Real Twine invited. "My house is so dope. Ha, ha, ha. My house is clean. Unfortunately, I'm supposed to be in another class right now. But I had to work overtime in here. I'll be back tomorrow." Ultimately, the work was uneven in sophistication, and students did not get to the point of incorporating a fuller variety of media, like podcasts, music or beats, or video. Videos, for example, could actually be shot inside this virtual world. But we found that we didn't have enough time for students to create these media at the same time that they were learning a wide range of fundamental skills needed for manipulating and experiencing Teen Second Life. One female student's frustration captured the problem of our time constraints. As Ms. Glide approached her work station she told her, "You see all this work I gotta do, Ms. Glide. You see all this work I gotta do to build this house? You know I don't really know what I'm doing."

To conclude this section, I briefly return to the development of one project from the unit, Terrance's performance space or club that was depicted at the beginning of the chapter. The process he went through in building it reflected a number of important considerations regarding the work these students did. Terrance was one of the students who really got into the project and, in Ms. Glide's words, "sped ahead." Like a number of the young men in the class, he wore dreads and wanted to put them on his avatar. "I need some dreads really quick," he said while creating it, asking, "Can you buy dreads?" But he was not able to. The person sitting next to him was the young woman who had expressed her frustration to Ms. Glide. As Terrance worked intently on his project, he also helped his station mate by guiding her through various steps in the process and patiently answering her questions. When she was trying to make walls, for example, he told her, "Look through the inventory for textures. Go all the way down to 'library.'"

Terrance talked to himself (or to his computer screen) a lot while he worked. "Alright, I got my floor down," he said out loud. Ms. Canon came over and looked at it. "Oh, that looks cool," she said. "I'm making a club," Terrance replied. He had initially started building a house but later became more excited about building a club space for different kinds of performances. "Are you going to put a pattern on your stage?" Ms. Canon asked. "Yeah, " he answered. "I gotta get everything coordinated, or I can't work with it." He thought for a while and then said to her, "I want to attach stuff. Can I upload some stuff?" "Like what?" she asked.

"Like some pictures. I have some of my pictures on Photoshop." They talked this over. It was one of the many instances of instructional conversations that occurred between the teachers and students. Students felt that this project was challenging, and they were able to get just-in-time consultations when they needed technical help or help with decisions about the content in their work. As a result of this conversation with Ms. Canon, Terrance decided to take some photos of himself and of his shirt with the Photo Booth application to upload onto his club, rather than to use pictures he had taken earlier and stored in Photoshop.

A bit later, the principal came in and watched Terrance work for a while. Finally, he asked what he was doing. "I'm working on my project," he said. "What I'm trying to do is get on there and get stuff up the way I want it. I want to have bulls running in the street." He continued working until the next class came in. Other students from the first class were still working on things, and several of them, including Terrance, asked to continue working during the next class. Ms. Canon came over and said, "Save your club, Terrance. Go into. . . . Oh, you're going to stay for the next class? Then when you're ready to go, let me know, and I'll make sure that you save everything." Most of the other students left, but Terrance stayed and continued working on his club. He eventually asked to keep working in Teen Second Life even after the unit of instruction ended.

During the next period, Ms. Canon checked on the progress that Terrance was making. "How's it going over here?" "Good." "Have you looked at all the textures?" she asked. "You might want the walls to have a different texture on the outside than on the inside." "Yeah, that's what I tryin' to do," Terrance said. They both studied the club for a while. "Sometimes you have to walk your avatar around it to get a better angle on it," she said as she left to check on someone else. As the project neared completion, Terrance created and hung a big blue ball from the ceiling and placed an even larger one in front of his stage. He later deleted the larger one, but he figured out how to animate the hanging ball, making it spin. "Cool," Ms. Canon said when she returned and saw what he had done. "I bet I could make this into a video game," Terrance said. "See the way I'm making this spin? I could make this into a video game." "You're right. They do use similar tools," she confirmed. They both seemed a little hypnotized by the spinning ball for a few moments. "This is a lot of work," Terrance said finally. "Its complicated, so complex. It takes time to get well into it. But it's fun."

LEARNING IN VIRTUAL WORLDS

"Is this some real stuff?" a student asked Ms. Canon on the first day of exploration in Teen Second Life. "Is it real?" she repeated. "It's virtual; but it's still real," Ms. Canon answered. Online multi-user virtual environments like Teen Second Life expand, complicate, and blur distinctions between stuff that is virtual and stuff that is real. MUVEs can be re-creations of physical worlds, completely imaginary worlds, or unique combinations of both, as is the case with Teen Second Life. Rather than attempting to ascribe borders between what is virtual and real, I think of virtual environments as providing alternative realities or choices for how one is able to experience reality. In MUVEs, these alternative realities occur in digitally mediated, three-dimensional, highly interactive, multi-user "places" that I believe must increasingly be present in schools.

"Place" is a fundamental concept in architecture and urban design that illuminates how possibilities for human activities are incorporated into or accommodated by the design of physical as well as virtual spaces. Because virtual spaces (like physical ones) are structured according to the uses and needs of humans, their designs extend from core principles that guide the designs of physical spaces. Human activities in both worlds have to be "situated" somewhere; they take place in a "place." Harrison and Dourish (1996) noted that "place" in a virtual world is not the three-dimensional space itself but, rather, derives (as it does in the physical world) from a tension between distinctiveness and connectedness. They argued,

> The critical property which designers are seeking, which we call appropriate behavioral framing, is not rooted in the properties of space at all. Instead, it is rooted in sets of mutually-held, and mutually available, cultural understandings about behavior and action. In contrast to "space," we call this a sense of "place." Our principle is: "Space is the opportunity; place is the understood reality." (67)

The school place is a distinctive reality that is in tension regarding its connectedness to the changing needs and interests of students and the changing realities of life beyond school. Incorporating new media more pervasively is not, in and of itself, a panacea for the critical problems impeding effective teaching and learning. However, ameliorating these problems begins with transforming how the reality of the school place can be reconceived. For this to happen, educators must redesign how behaviors and activities are framed and enacted, to better leverage the backgrounds, experiences, interests, and cultural understandings of students as foundations and sources for high intellectual performances that are viably connected to the world beyond school. This world and student experiences in it are increasingly represented in and realized though digital media. I believe that the unit in Teen Second Life emitted glimmers of possibilities for new realities in the place that we call school.

For a number of reasons, Ms. Glide could not have instituted this curricular unit without the support of members of the TEACH Project and the work of Ms. Canon in particular. It was reminiscent of how Ms. Young was integral to the work in the first semester of Ms. Foster's class. Perhaps this indicates the need to have a technology coordinator on site at schools as a central component of the overall educational mission. But it should also be remembered that without Ms. Young in the second semester, Ms. Foster continued to extend the uses of technology in her classes as her own confidence and competence grew through her teaching practices. This was a reflection of how teachers needed to continually develop by engaging in new learning themselves.

Ms. Glide became an example of a teacher who was continually engaged in learning that was new, in the Teen Second Life unit and afterward in her teaching practice. During the professional development sessions, she and other teachers were guided on downloading Second Life, building their own avatars, and practicing the basic movements, navigation skills, and communicative capabilities of the program. This was partially why she felt comfortable attempting the unit with her class. Her changing understanding of her practice continued after this unit that took place toward the end of the school year. For example, she wrote to me with an outline of a project that she wanted to do during the summer with some of her students: "I've been thinking about trying to pioneer some kind of class during the summer that would allow me and my students to work remotely—some kind of electronic blackboard or blog site. The idea would be to have students working continuously on digital projects and using technology to give them immediate feedback. I feel like it could continue some of the work that we started in spring semester."

Ms. Glide had seen that the dynamics of her class had changed dramatically while the unit was going on, and she wanted to continue the students' development as well as hers. I have described earlier how their projects had been realized in individual and joint productive activity that distributed the learning as well as the accountability and support for learning among and between the students and their teachers. These activities revealed students' successes and challenges in creating complex virtual artifacts and collaborating in real time with peers and adults. The students' learning also reflected significant forms of academic discourse. I discussed how there was considerable expertise in Ms. Glide's class itself as the students learned and also helped each other. For example, there were the interesting contributions of Jada, who actually led instruction and even answered an occasional technical question from Ms. Canon.

Although mediating teaching and learning with technology can be challenging, that should not stymie educators in leveraging its affordances. With an understanding that there will always be technical problems and concerns, it was important to consider the ways that teaching and learning significantly changed during this unit. Within the digitally mediated context of Teen Second Life, the sense of place was not only distinctive; it also offered dynamic possibilities for connectedness that was culturally grounded (often in youth popular culture), on the one hand, yet interestingly linked to a range of real-world activities, on the other.

In an article on critical media literacy, Sholle and Denski (1993) argued that "educational theory must engage with the popular as the background that informs students' engagement with any pedagogical encounter" (307). In this chapter, I have attempted to show that despite its constraints, work in Teen Second Life enabled a wide range of personal and popular cultural content and connections to learning and activities that were challenging and complex. The point was not to valorize the students' personal interests and cultural contexts but to enable connections to aspects of their prior knowledge as a part of their processes for learning. With more time, the overall focus of the curriculum could have been easily infused with (or aligned with) more direct disciplinary content and more specific driving questions that could have been generated by the teachers and the students. But even with the limits of the unit, it was clear that work in virtual environments could provide a fertile context to support active, critical inquiry and project-based, participatory learning. I think it is also clear that educators must take advantage of emerging technologies that have capabilities to immerse students within contexts that challenge, ground, and ultimately extend their understandings.

The students' connectedness to the symbolic texts and to the constructed reality of the virtual world of Teen Second Life was revealed in part through the high levels of excitement and enjoyment that characterized the engagement of almost every student that worked with the unit. Ms. Glide was impressed by the fact that attendance increased dramatically during the unit. She had never before seen her students lobby to stay and work during second period for the class or to continue working on their projects after school. At times, she had to turn away students from other classes who tried to sit in during these periods in the computer lab and join in the work her students were doing. "You guys get to play a game in class?" they would ask. For sure, there were also problems, which will be discussed in the concluding chapter. Yet each day was generally marked by student experiences of delight, discovery, and dedication to the work of producing digital images and objects and to communicating and learning with others in both virtual and physical worlds.

Among other things, the script or narrative of this MUVE positioned and reinforced the identities of students as producers with the agency, power, and tools to design and build all sorts of things, beginning with their avatars and continuing to a wide range of objects with varying complexities. Their building, travel, and communicative activities encouraged or required that they probe the multimodal affordances of the virtual environment through their avatars and decode meanings in an array of semiotic domains. Bugeja (2007) noted, "The conscience responds to symbols as if they were real. Avatars symbolize the self. They represent our deepest wishes, aspirations, virtues, and yes, vices. Nothing is more authentic." The students' experiences were not only real; they also represented significant learning that had obvious as well as subtle links to learning and experiences beyond the alternative realities of Teen Second Life.

I now offer a closing reflection on this learning with a final reference to the club that Terrance built. A video posted on YouTube that highlighted activities in Second Life depicted a New York–styled loft placed there by Warner Brothers to promote singer/pianist Regina Spektor. If you go to this loft in Second Life, your avatar could animate prompts that would provide news, a photo gallery, audio and video clips, and tour dates for this popular singer. There were interesting correspondences between this loft space and the club space that Terrance built. He had imaginatively placed photos of himself in his club in ways that provided a culturally specific personalization of the design. Although he ran out of time, his intention was to build more things into the space like a photo gallery and prompts to play his favorite music in addition to enabling it to host performances of hip-hop music, dance, and the spoken word. With more time, he could have also actualized his desire to "have bulls running in the street."

In probing what the virtual environment enabled him to build, Terrance saw how it could be used to create video games. "See, that's how they make video games," he said at one point in his building process. In fact, there are games that have been designed and played in Teen Second Life. Some are role-playing games that use imaginary characters or pop culture characters like those from the *Star Wars* movies. In his book *How Computer Games Help Children Learn,* Shaffer (2006) argued that modeling epistemic, role-playing games on the work and skills used in actual professions would be a powerful design for teaching and learning in schools. A video game called SL-ingo that focused on allowing for quick action on fast-changing information displayed multidimensionally was designed and perfected in Second Life and then licensed to a real business. So there were clear connections to important skills and perspectives in the world beyond school in the kinds of probing of material intelligence built into the digital environment by Terrance, which reflected active, critical learning that had links to some level of his prior knowledge and interests.

Essentially, what both Warner Brothers and Terrance had done in building loft and club spaces was to use computational tools to enact designs that would give digital spaces a sense of place. They utilized opportunities provided in digital worlds to put unique understandings and experiences into place. Their designs differentially incorporated or accommodated a variety of "real" human activities, one of which is engaged learning. As Terrance said, "It's complicated, so complex. It takes time to get well into it. But it's fun."

5 | A SECOND LIFE FOR LEARNING

With ever-expanding modes for making meaning, creating and enacting identities and social networking enabled by digital media, the roles and challenges of teachers are more crucial than ever. Consequently, the professional development of teachers has to activate instructional leadership that addresses the immediate dynamics of classroom practices and problems while simultaneously supporting and guiding teachers to imagine and implement new practices that effectively utilize appropriate, emerging digital resources for learning, communication, and creative production. This does not necessarily mean that earlier approaches and traditions will become obsolete. But the work of teachers themselves should make pivotal contributions to the new directions taken in the uses of technology for teaching and learning in order to best connect to, alter, or extend prior approaches to better serve the changing needs of students and society.

In line with these perspectives, the TEACH Project worked to facilitate and support teachers in leadership roles in their professional development. In the PD sessions, teachers were positioned not only to learn with each other but also to lead each other in learning about how to implement digital projects with students in their classes. In the process, with a particular focus on the classes of two teachers (Ms. Foster and Ms. Glide), we supported, observed, and documented ways that teaching practices changed through incorporating more technology into instruction. We also observed and documented ways that their students' learning changed in connection with these changing teaching practices. Additionally, we assessed a number of obstacles and challenges encountered by both teachers and students as they worked to improve the quality of teaching and learning in the intricate context of the continuation high school.

In this final chapter, I first review key obstacles and challenges in this school setting. Next, I consider the productive changes that occurred during the project with respect to the students' learning despite these obstacles. Then I discuss vital aspects of the teachers' learning that occurred during the project. In addressing the learning of students and teachers, I make connections to principles of learning with new media (Gee 2004) and to principles of effective teaching from CREDE (Stoddart 2005) that guided the implementation of the TEACH Project. I also make connections to the National Educational Technology Standards for teachers and students that are emerging in the United States (see the appendixes in this book and International Society for Technology in Education 2008). Finally, I discuss implications for teaching and learning beyond the context of this unique urban school.

OBSTACLES TO LEARNING

At the beginning of the second week of the Second Life unit in Ms. Glide's World Media class, an African American male student who I had never seen in the class before walked into the computer lab. "Ms. Glide, how long do I have to be in your class?" he asked. She saw that he was already agitated. "From two to three," she replied. "Is that all we gonna do is be on the computer for an hour?" he continued. "I don't like that! That's why I be leaving. These classes are too long." Ms. Glide talked with the young man about what we were doing in the unit, and he settled down before long to begin working on the project. However, he soon became frustrated because the computer he was working on was moving very slowly.

Beyond problems with the technology itself, this scene marked issues of attendance and disaffection as clear obstacles to this student's opportunity to learn. Too often the typical practices of schooling define these problems as mainly residing within students themselves—the so-called oppositional personality that Ogbu (2003) and others have described at length. Yet we understood that critical challenges to students' as well as teachers' learning originated in larger structures and cultures of schooling in our society. I discussed some of the issues related to problematic aspects of schooling in this country in the first chapter, so here I will emphasize only a few things related to ways that students like those at V-Tech were pushed to the margins. I also address a bit more of the limits of teacher training in the effective use of technology.

In light of the myriad obstacles that their students faced, the teachers, administrators, and staff at V-Tech were committed to implementing its "three R's": "relationships," "rigor," and "relevance." Ms. Glide's interaction with the disaffected student was a partial example of this. Yet the substance of many marginalized students' experiences in schools does not reflect any one of these three R's. Most often, they are not enabled through productive relationships with teachers and peers in conjunction with high expectations for rigorous work and productive behavior, though we know that high expectations of rigor for all students result in higher academic success. Students like those at V-Tech don't usually see much relevance, particularly in terms of their cultural backgrounds, in much of what they have been asked to learn during their time in school. In many cases, schools primarily use discipline structures to address disaffection and defiance, despite their roots in other situational obstacles to learning. Then they create continuation schools that mainly work to isolate these students and further exacerbate the obstacles to learning they face. The work at V-Tech, as this book has shown, was exceptional in this regard.

Substantial research links low expectations for behavior and lack of cultural understanding to wide-ranging and frequently inequitable discipline practices (Gregory, Nygreen, and Moran 2006; Noguera 1995, 2003; Witt 2007). Witt (2007) analyzed comprehensive, state-by-state data collected by the U.S. Department of Education for the 2004–5 school year. He found that on average across all of the states in the nation, African American students are expelled at nearly three times the rate of white students. This expansive data also showed that African American students are not any more likely to misbehave than other students from the same socioeconomic backgrounds, yet they are punished more severely and more frequently than others for the same offenses (Witt 2007).

Noguera (1995) argued that the essence of many school approaches to discipline is the identification and segregation of "problem" students—separating the "bad kids" from the "good kids." Yet, as Gregory, Nygreen, and Moran (2006) note, "such practices invariably reinforce stereotypes about 'good kids' and 'bad kids' and end up reproducing the same inequalities they were put in place to counteract" (145). They also remove responsibility from teachers and staff for reengaging these students in learning. Instead, teachers who may have begun their careers intending to be caring and stimulating fall into what Haberman (2006) described as a "pedagogy of poverty," which includes acts of traditional urban teaching like giving information, asking questions, making assignments, monitoring seatwork, reviewing assignments, giving tests, assigning homework, reviewing homework, marking papers, giving grades, and punishing noncompliance. The most extreme consequence of this kind of teaching, short of the students actually dropping out of high school, is their placement in continuation high schools that are prevalent throughout the country. According to Noguera (2003), these "punishment" schools become holding places for students who are deemed a threat to the education and safety of others, and he asserts that it is not coincidental that they come from the most difficult personal and social circumstances.

The predominantly African American and Latino students at V-Tech have experienced various combinations of these practices that have just been described. For compelling reasons, these students interpret and internalize their experiences with these schooling practices as being intricately linked to race—an aspect of inequitable differences in achievement that is simultaneously visible and veiled. So the obstacles to learning that are addressed in this section must be considered within this context of issues that have consequences for learning that can be at least as profound as the impacts of pedagogy and curriculum.

In addition to these structural issues, there were also a number of site-specific obstacles to students' learning at V-Tech. Despite the school community's commitment to its students, attendance was continually a problem for every class in the school. Not only would the students that were present on a given day not reflect the actual number in a class, but there would often be different groupings of the students each day. This problem was increased due to the fact that the main high school sent new students to V-Tech every week. Sometimes students would not attend due to lack of interest in what was going on in classes. They might even come and check on what was going on and then decide not to stay. As one student said after spending a few minutes in a class, "I'm 'bout to leave. I'm bored. School's gettin' boring." On one occasion, this occurred even during Ms. Glide's unit in the computer lab. A student that had not been present for a couple of days walked into the lab and said, "You all still working in Second Life. Why y'all doing that nonsense?"

But there were numerous other reasons for students being absent, due to problems they were encountering in their lives beyond school. For example, many would often change addresses frequently as their home situations changed. Many students had to work for a significant number of hours each week to help support their families or to support themselves. Sometimes there were traumatic events occurring in their lives, as alluded to in some of the podcasts that were created in Ms. Foster's Hip-Hop Journalism class. At times, cell phones would ring in class, and students sometimes felt they needed to go out of the room to take the calls, because emergencies often occurred.

Problems with the use of technology itself also caused obstacles to learning and significant frustration for students and teachers alike. At times, the wireless connections would be down, or the MUVE itself would be down or moving very slowly or would require (as was the case with Teen Second Life) complicated processes for getting logged on. If a student was not able to complete the registration process all at one time, for example, she or he would have to start over from the beginning the next time. Telephone numbers were supposed to be used as part of the registration process, and some students did not have either cell phones or home phones. Additionally, as earlier noted, the principal had to initially get that site unblocked for use in the school before the program could be downloaded on the computers in the lab.

Some computers worked better than others, some would crash often, and some just needed repairs. Because of attendance or the uneven pace of digital work, students would be at very different places in their work on assigned projects. For example, one student exclaimed to the class, "You all building housing and stuff, and I can't even log in." Of course, at times, some students would get off task surfing to other websites or playing music or other games on their computers. Consequently, strategies were needed to harness students' creative divergences. Sometimes, however, music would be heard that was a part of a site in Teen Second Life. So music that was on task was sometimes hard to distinguish from other music that might be heard. On task or not, just the sounds of different music could cause dissonance during the unit. In one case, a girl tried to mediate between two others by saying, "Why don't both of you turn your music down? Let's act like we're in high school!" Because of the modular nature of work in the computer labs, there would also be multiple conversations going on most of the time, and the teachers could not completely monitor if they were always focused on the work.

Although, among other things, the project was designed to support the teachers' professional development with the use of technology, it was clear that they did not have effective training in this area in their teacher preparation programs. So another obstacle to learning with new media was the need to change the teachers' perspectives about teaching and to get beyond a certain amount of reliance on and comfort with more traditional methods. The teachers reported very little, if any, training from their teacher preparation or PD programs prior to V-Tech for integrating technology effectively into instruction. Getting beyond the reliance on page-based methods required more than just increasing the teachers' technological proficiency. It required a fundamental shift in their perspectives about teaching, and these kinds of shifts are often difficult to make. One reason that we began with the teaching principles from CREDE was to facilitate considerations of redesigning classrooms and instruction whether it utilized digital technologies or not. Use of things like activity centers, joint productivity activities, instructional conversations, and project-based learning were modeled and encouraged during the first semester to help teachers see possibilities for new dynamics in the nature of learning activities in the classroom.

So one way of thinking about the obstacles to learning had to do with the problems of changing the culture of schooling relative to how teachers have been prepared to teach, particularly with urban students. Stigler and Hiebert (1999) documented not only that the United States prepared teachers in less effective ways compared to other nations but that their preparation was also much more generic and did not give significant account to some of the unique challenges of urban schools. Consequently, in addition to structural issues noted earlier, the traditional culture of teaching, which often is not questioned or critiqued by those who transmit or enact it, was a pervasive obstacle to the transformation of learning in the school.

STUDENTS' LEARNING

For the TEACH Project, student learning was predicated on teachers effectively incorporating the students' backgrounds, experiences, interests, and cultural perspectives into the curriculum. We felt that the use of digital tools was a powerful and potentially exciting way to link these considerations to the students' learning and allow greater receptivity to diverse learning styles. This kind of learning occurred throughout the project despite the obstacles discussed in the previous section. In this section, I primarily use considerations of the work that took place in the classes of the two focal teachers to delineate essential characteristics of changes in the students' learning. I also illustrate how their students' learning was connected to a number of principles of learning associated with new media (Gee 2004) as well as how it reflected key aspects of the emerging National Educational Technology Standards (NETS) for student work. These standards were published in June 2008, the month our PD sessions ended, yet they offer useful frameworks for considering our students' and teachers' learning with technology.

The most important thing that characterized the learning of the students as a result of changing teaching practices during the TEACH Project was reflected in the first learning principle that Gee (2004) put forth: active, critical learning. This principle was powerfully revealed through the digitally mediated, project-based work in the Hip-Hop Journalism class taught by Ms. Foster and Ms. Young. Enacting this fundamental change also engaged other key learning principles that Gee outlined. It encouraged the students to develop inquiry-learning processes that required "probing" the "semiotic domains" of "designed" environments to "discover" their built-in resources for learning and making meaning (i.e., their "material intelligence," or what I called the "third participant"). In so doing, students could get the information, ideas, images, sounds, or animations needed to more deeply understand issues, problems, or challenges and to create ideas, digital objects, and products that reflected their learning. These characteristics of the students' learning were also highly consistent with ways that the six key NETS for students emphasize the use of digital tools to promote specific kinds of critical thinking, creativity, communication and collaboration, citizenship, research, information fluency, and skill in the use of technology systems.

Through Ms. Foster's use of project-based activities, her students created youth commentaries and podcasts, digital stories and PowerPoint presentations, photography projects and blogs, and digital beats and lyrics. During these activities, they learned how to make meaning in and critique a variety of textual mediums, including written texts, as well as how to go back and forth between writing and electronic communication. One example of the convergence of a number of the principles of learning outlined by Gee was in the magazine project, where students brought together multiple sign systems—words, images, symbols, and artifacts—in a complex semiotic domain that blended traditional literacies of essay and story writing with the construction of complementary digital images and objects. They developed expertise in computer applications like Photoshop and Photo Booth and learned to capture, manipulate, and repurpose visual texts from Internet sources like Google Images. In line with the NETS for students, these young people were encouraged to "create original works" using "a variety of digital environments and media" to "interact, collaborate, and publish with peers, experts, or others" and, in the process, used their "existing knowledge to generate new ideas" and "construct knowledge."

Through being positioned as journalists, the students learned about the workings of the journalism field as one model for accessing and producing knowledge, and they learned ways that this field and others were being transformed by affordances of new media. For instance, they were able to conduct research and do Internet searches in the process of creating digital and written texts that reflected their voices, perspectives, and critiques on issues that were local, national, and international. Consistent with the NETS for information fluency, this required them to "locate, organize, analyze, evaluate, synthesize, and ethically use information from a variety of sources and media."

When some of these issues were potentially traumatic or hit particularly close to home for students, like racial profiling or the Jena Six situation, Ms. Foster felt that the students' work with digital tools made discussions of the critical social issues and events more viable. She found that addressing and presenting on these issues with digital media changed the communication dynamic and allowed students to appreciate and gain comfort with new possibilities for telling their own stories and providing critiques about social issues and conditions that affected their lives. This was revealed in ways that students presented their projects to others in the class as well as to the larger community and, ultimately, the world by utilizing digital media to communicate unique cultural perspectives and material. At times, the effect was subtle, as with Rosa's gaining confidence through her PowerPoint presentation to talk in front of the class about her family's experiences with racial profiling. At times, it was more dramatic, as with Jalen's podcast about how he suffered from something akin to post-traumatic stress syndrome as a result of the violence he had experienced in his life or DeShawn's use of a blog site as his "world wide wall" to, among other things, honor a fallen friend. Students noted that they liked how the class was about real stuff instead of boring stuff that didn't affect them. These kinds of class projects connected directly to the NETS for students to use appropriate digital tools and resources to "identify and define authentic problems and significant questions for investigation" and to employ "multiple processes and diverse perspectives to explore alternative solutions."

Through the work in Ms. Foster's class, students became excited and highly focused about learning. There was often laughter and other signs of genuine enjoyment. Sometimes students stayed after class or worked through breaks on the projects. Some took on leadership roles or roles as peer pedagogues. Many found that they could be more independent as learners while also learning in collaboration and dialogue with each other, the smart tools, and their teachers. Ms. Foster was even able to use digital tools to keep students like Darius plugged in to class activities during periods when he was not able to come to school. In some cases, her students were stimulated to go beyond class assignments in order to learn more about things like the history behind computers or how to do higher-level graphic or sound designs. They also understood more about the processes and importance of doing research to inform themselves and others about social and global issues. They were being reconnected to learning through both the digital and the social supports that Ms. Foster employed. More and more, they came to appreciate their individual strengths and interests as they experienced how learning could be serious fun and also relevant to their present and possible lives.

In Ms. Glide's unit focused in Teen Second Life, student learning was also engaging and challenging. More so than in Ms. Foster's class, student learning during the unit took place in three-dimensional, virtual spaces. Also, the products of their projects existed primarily as digital texts. Students had to confront new considerations of identity, including their identities as learners, through novel connections between the virtual and the real, the mind and the body, space and place, and production and consumption that came into play in novel expressive modes. In fact, their acts of identity construction—their connection of the academic demands to personal interests—were central to the learning that took place during this unit. The Doe Magic and BigO Footman avatars were not only fun or culturally configured choices; their realization marked the development of beginning computational literacy skills that would be continually built on for more complex learning activities. Construction of avatars and eventually other objects required students to reflect on their multiple real-world and virtual identities as they traveled to virtual places that linked and overlapped subjective and collective digital realities. Lave (1998) noted how this kind of learning is stretched across mind, body, activity, and culturally organized settings, and a similar stretching occurs with digitized bodies, activities, and cultural settings.

With regard to the learning principles enabled by digital media as noted by Gee (2004, 207–11), Ms. Glide's students learned, by enacting virtual identities, to "probe" the alternative realities and reflect on the consequences of their actions. This is how Terrance discovered that affordances in the design of Teen Second Life could also be used to create unique video games. The consequences of probing actions offered or required choices for subsequent actions that guided incremental increases in learning and skill development related to the challenges of the virtual environment. For example, Saysay Snoodie engaged in extended discussions with Ms. Canon to learn how to implement her selections in constructing a more visually nuanced avatar. Through the "incremental principle" in this virtual environment, learning situations were ordered in the early stages so that they built on "intuitive knowledge," such that earlier experiences led to understandings that were fruitful for addressing more complex situations and challenges. From this perspective, the students' learning involved developing increasing levels of mastery of the "semiotic domains" of Teen Second Life—the interrelations of meanings within and across multiple sign systems—through increasing levels of participation. This kind of learning was not only "distributed" across the learner, the virtual objects and symbols, and the digital tools; it was also able to be transferred to relatable situations, issues, conditions, or challenges in the real world beyond the virtual model.

Ms. Foster and Ms. Young modeled the production of digital projects for their students. In Ms. Glide's classes, students' development of understanding and proficiency with specific computational literacy skills was through a process of model building in which the initial objects that they had to build modeled the building of all digital objects and structures of varying or increasing complexity. In this unit, they experienced a process of learning in which performance occurred before (and en route to) competence. As Jada built more and more elaborate houses and as Terrance elaborated his loft space, their learning was linked to their increasing capabilities for system manipulations and to the just-in-time solutions they needed to face the changing challenges. The sixth standard of the NETS for students addresses exactly these competencies to effectively use technology systems and applications. Additionally, all of the students were learning more about specific real-world activities and professions that related to various activities in the virtual world, consistent with Shaffer's (2006) argument about the epistemic possibilities of role-playing games.

As Ms. Foster's students learned about social issues and events taking place in the physical world, Ms. Glide's students traveled, learned in, and ultimately built their own additions to the virtual world. Intuitively, they instantiated a sense of place in the objects and structures that they built, but they also had to confront the visible and visceral duplicity of identities, including their identities as learners, as they transformed into cyberbodies and traveled in cyberspace. In addition to learning computational literacies, Ms. Glide's students learned to ground their identities by creating imagined places that were nonetheless culturally defined. Yet they were also intellectually and culturally challenged by their travels and encounters with other avatars and other realities, in ways that were consistent with the NETS for developing understanding and global awareness by engaging other cultures. Along the way, they learned more about their strengths as they worked in unique situations, met unusual challenges, and had to manage their frustrations in order to complete their virtual projects. They also learned more about collaborative work, as they both needed support in their work and were able to give support to the work of others in the class, consistent with the NETS for utilizing digital tools to work collaboratively.

Students even saw one of their peers, Jada, emerge as a capable "expert" who could lead part of the instruction as effectively as their teachers could. This echoed the expertise of Deja in the magazine project, with her skills and instruction leadership with digital photography. It also echoed the work of DeShawn, who became a recognized expert through the creation of his blog that he called the "world wide wall." Despite some constraints and obstacles to learning in the unit in Ms. Glide's class, the students' work in Teen Second Life enabled a range of cultural content and connections to learning and activities that were complex and challenging. With the exception of a couple of students, she noted, "most students had really positive things to say about the experience."

Intense interest and excitement were also clear characteristics of the students' learning with digital tools. Although the work in Ms. Foster and Ms. Glide's classes was mainly focused on their class subjects, the students' enthusiasm also spilled over into other teachers' classes. For example, there were times when students asked other teachers if they could use blogs, podcasts, or other kinds of digital texts in conjunction with the work they were doing in other classes. At times, this caused teachers to collaborate with each other on assignments that went across specific disciplines in the school. It also motivated students to sometimes try to join in on classes in which they were not enrolled, because they had heard about or seen the digitally mediated learning that was going on.

TEACHERS' LEARNING

At the end of the school year, the teachers were interviewed about what they felt they learned and gained from the PD project. Although they all gained greater understanding and considerable experience with the value, uses, and range of digital tools available for instruction (as reflected in chapter 3), their confidence and competence in actually mediating student learning with digital technology were uneven. To capture more of what was possible in terms of the learning of students at the school, I highlighted work in Ms. Foster and Ms. Glide's classes. In this section, I discuss key characteristics of the V-Tech teachers' learning with the understanding that there were differential levels of comfort in their attempts to implement what they were learning about uses of technology in instruction over the course of the academic year.

It was important that the teachers learned new perspectives about teaching as well as new teaching practices. Obviously, the two go hand in hand, yet the CREDE standards were important for teaching with or without high levels of technology use. Importantly, work with the CREDE standards helped change perspectives on teaching in ways that facilitated possibilities for greater use of digital tools. In other words, specific knowledge and skills with technology were only part of what was needed for effective instruction. The pedagogical knowledge that teachers needed to implement the CREDE standards was also crucial. For example, in his math class, Mr. Guy used joint productive activities and instructional dialogues for challenging and complex tasks in trigonometry that also connected across disciplines to his students' prior knowledge and experiences, all in conjunction with the digital affordances of Google Earth. The perspective on joint productive activities along with project-based learning, in fact, undergirded our PD approach and allowed us to focus the teachers' learning on their actual work in classrooms. Yet, since very little use of digital tools was going on in most of the teachers' classrooms, there also had to be a balance of addressing learning to use various digital tools in the PD sessions and then attempting to support their implementation in the teachers' practices. This was the key challenge—the actual implementation of what the teachers were learning.

In this regard, Ms. Church noted, "I feel like I'm that teacher who doesn't get any of this into the classroom. I still feel apprehensive. I just like to be in my classroom where I can control how things go." Yet she did actively try some things to change her practice, as she indicated later: "Still, I use other innovations. I still feel like blogs are the most key things that we have tried, and I also had the senior project do some online components as one of the things that they can do to have different presentation modes. But I'm still reluctant to take that plunge into something like Second Life." This last point was understandable since the use of that virtual environment for instruction required intensive support. Yet the principal captured the way we hoped we would help the teachers learn to change their practice when he said, in one of the PD sessions, that it really was not about learning isolated applications: "It's really about imagining the kinds of things you want students to create and thinking about the design and intersection of the kinds of applications that will allow them to do these things."

The following teacher comments reflect how they felt about their learning through the PD program over the course of the academic year. Every teacher was impressed by the capabilities of the wide range of digital media that they learned about and worked with during the PD sessions, and they were excited by many of the possibilities they held for mediating and motivating student learning. But at the end of the school year, a few of the teachers, like Mr. Roy, who taught science, still felt "technology challenged." He stated, for example, "I'm still kinda intimidated by all the techno aspects of everything."

The responses of the eight teachers ranged from Mr. Roy's continuing sense of feeling intimidated by the use of technology in his classes to Ms. Foster's eager embrace and experimentation with almost every digital tool that we introduced. She noted, "I've really gotten a lot out of the professional development. And I continue to bring technology into my classes and use techniques that I pretty much learned from this PD." Mr. Elder remained closer to the position of Mr. Roy regarding technology. He felt that he had "gotten quite a bit out of [professional development]" and had "learned how to use [computers] more as an asset inside the classroom." But his main uses in his math classes during the year were administrative. Ms. Rivers thought that even some administrative uses of new media could have pedagogical purposes. For example, she felt that her keeping a class blog to post course content and assignments really helped some of her students with inconsistent attendance keep up enough to get passing grades. Ms. Kim, one of the English teachers, tried some pedagogical uses of what she learned about a few digital tools, but she noted, "I have mostly done Internet research with the students when they have to write a paper." Her fellow English teacher, Ms. Church, worked to incorporate more of the digital tools that she learned about in the PD sessions into her instruction. She noted, "This year I've noticed that I just feel a lot more equipped. Um, all the different ideas that I've seen and some I tried, like using technology, using audio, GarageBand, podcasting." Mr. Guy, the math teacher, also was quite comfortable using digital tools in his teaching, and he made an interesting breakthrough with the use of Google Earth to teach trigonometry. Although Ms. Glide started out quite intimidated by the thought of using technology in her classes, the PD sessions helped her gain the confidence to experiment with almost as many digital tools as Ms. Foster. For example, Ms. Glide stated,

> I would say that I would be one of those teachers who was not tech savvy and not interested in using technology. But as I was going through the PD, I started incorporating a lot of the applications right into my classes while it was still fresh to me. I did a unit on child soldiers in Africa, and I had the students using Google Earth to kind of understand the geographical components of where all of this was taking place. Students would have to make critical judgments based on their use of the technology. For example, if we were looking for a particular village that child soldiers came from and couldn't find it using Google Earth, students would have to figure out things like was the village so small that it couldn't be seen, or did it get destroyed in the war? I had them set up blogs and make entries using the CIA *Factbook* and evaluating that as a resource. Using these different media helped the students, I think, see themselves more as global citizens.

I include Ms. Glide's extended statement here to connect the uses of technology by some of the V-Tech teachers to key considerations from the five NETS for teachers. One of these new technology standards for teachers was to "design or adapt relevant learning experiences that incorporate digital tools and resources to promote student learning and creativity." Another related technology standard was for teachers to "develop technology-enriched learning environments that enable all students to pursue their individual curiosities." I selected these two standards from the NETS because they go to the core of teachers' need to utilize technology to support the diverse needs of learners, on the one hand, and to maximize the learning of all students, on the other. Ms. Glide's work as she described it (as well as the work of most of the teachers in the yearlong project) was definitely moving toward the goals of these standards in how technology was being incorporated into instruction. Another one of the standards addresses the need for teachers to use technology with their students to enhance their global awareness. In Ms. Glide's work as well as in the work of other V-Tech teachers that has been reported throughout this book, various digital tools were used to extend the students' learning to global issues and events. These were clear ways that learning to use technology helped the teachers change their teaching practices and perspectives to more effectively engage and increase the learning of their students.

Critical challenges that the teachers faced as they learned and worked to utilize more technology were dramatically portrayed as they reflected on the school year that was ending and projected on the new year coming. For example, although Mr. Roy did not feel he had been successful in implementing things he was learning in the PD sessions, he was nonetheless enthusiastic about increasing his use of technology in the next academic year.

> I was able to accomplish a few things, and I really enjoyed it [the professional development]. What really inspired me is that some of the students took some of the things that we did in class with the other teachers, who were better with the technology than me, and the students really enjoyed it. And it really hit home that I have to get my act together as far as technology is concerned if I really want to be a twenty-first-century teacher. So I'm taking this to heart, and over the summer I'm going to improve on my Second Life, and improve on a lot of other things so that I can inspire the students. A lot of them have a lot of issues. And one of the issues that they don't have is dealing with technology. So I really need to get it together, and I hope to encourage them and inspire them to become better science students.

All of the teachers saw that the learning of V-Tech students was being revitalized through the use of technology, even when it was occurring in classes other than their own. Ms. Kim, for example, felt that it was great to be exposed to so many new ideas about teaching while, at the same time, having a continuing forum for learning how to implement these ideas and link them to teaching standards.

> Working in professional development with the technology is good. It's good to think about how you could use technology. It's always nice when you have new ideas. It's kind of a challenge, because then you think, well,

there are all these standards you have to meet, and how can the two merge.
. . . But I think it will be cool next year to have more web resources . . . and
also having the students have a blog and having them comment on maybe a
book that we are reading at the time. So I definitely think that it's been
useful to have that time in PD to bounce ideas off of people when the
ideas strike.

Ms. Kim's comments indicate the challenges of making the work with
technology connect to traditional teaching standards, yet the V-Tech
teachers were able to make those connections in interesting ways. I have
also shown how their work directly connected to key emerging standards
that are being adopted for teaching with technology, although these
standards were not published early enough to be incorporated into our
PD project. Ms. Kim also touched on one of the most important things
that the teachers understood from their experiences of working together
during the year—the value and vitality of their close, extended collaborations with each other in facilitating and motivating their learning.
Another example of a new vitality for the learning of V-Tech teachers as
well as for the learning of their students was provided by Ms. Church as
she reflected on the closing and coming school years.

> I will say that this year has been dramatically better for me than last year.
> Last year was my first year of teaching. Teaching at this school in par-
> ticular. And it was really difficult. At the end of last year, I was a lot more
> stressed and a little disappointed in myself. But this year I've noticed that I
> just feel a lot more equipped. Um, all the different ideas that I've seen and
> some I tried, like using technology, using audio, GarageBand, podcast-
> ing—I feel like those are really cutting-edge things. And I feel like if we can
> make them work here at this school, then we have some limitless possibili-
> ties before us. . . . And I just feel, like, a lot more energetic about teaching.
> And I don't feel the same way that I felt before when I was questioning
> if I would even come back. Like right now, I'm in there. I'm excited! Just
> the kind of energy and motivation that I have gotten from some of the
> ideas I've gotten this year. And the talk about collaborating with the game
> school on the East Coast. So I appreciate all of these kinds of conversations
> that we have been able to have.

Obviously, teaching in a continuation school was extremely challenging, and these challenges exacted tolls on teachers and students

alike. Yet, like Ms. Church, the teachers at V-Tech finished the school year feeling quite encouraged about their work to change their teaching practices and with high hopes for going further with this in the coming year. For example, Ms. Rivers noted that she felt much better about her experiences during the school year and her future teaching prospects at the school than she did about all of her former teaching experiences.

> This is my fourth year of teaching, and it's been the first year that I have enjoyed teaching. So this has been a great year for me. The collegiality, the administrative support—I felt very supported, and for that reason it's been fabulous. And I actually now look forward to next year. I've never looked forward to the next year before. Having professional development centered around technology and giving us tools to become better teachers, I actually fell in line with the whole objective of supporting teachers. So I appreciated it. Even if I'm not going to be able to implement everything right now or if I don't use everything that we learned, I implemented some of the things. . . . But I like the fact that we were offered these technologies as our professional development, because it obviously has the potential to relieve our pressure and help us be better teachers.

Clearly, teachers are most often under intense pressure in nearly every educational context. The use of technology alone will not mitigate that pressure or necessarily result in effective teaching. However, insights from the teachers at V-Tech regarding their experiences in learning to incorporate technology into their instruction, albeit at widely varying levels, illustrated that despite the pressures and obstacles of teaching, new life was brought to the learning of students and teachers that was relevant and rigorous but also predicated on productive relationships. Ms. Foster, a sterling teacher and leader at the school, provided one final, powerful consideration of the PD work and collaborations over the year.

> It's been a hard year professionally, but even more so for me personally. [For one thing, her laptop was stolen during the second semester.] Yet I've really gotten a lot out of the professional development, and I continue to bring tech into my classes and use techniques that I pretty much learned from this PD. I'm excited about Word. Sound. Life [a new application that Mr. Cameron developed]. I think that's going to be a good addition to my classes. So I'm really looking forward to using that next year. I really have enjoyed working with the other teachers and staff. I love each and every one of them. That's been what's kept me grounded. I think some collaboration has started to kinda pick up, but it's kind of been organic. When we

come together even more purposefully in a more organized kind of way, I think it's going to be even better. So I look forward to collaborating with my peers.

Ms. Foster was essentially saying that the personal and professional relationships and collaborations were key and that the school community needed to continue developing in this area as the foundation for achieving other goals, including our goals for increasing the use of technology. She concluded that in her own quest for professional development, "I just feel like it's those personal transformations for me as a teacher that make the technology so worthwhile and so important."

IMPLICATIONS FOR SCHOOLING

The TEACH Project's PD work with V-Tech teachers and the teachers' concurrent work with students had a number of implications for changing perspectives and practices of schooling. These implications not only relate to reengaging students who are having critical academic or discipline problems in schools; they also reflect ways to effectively prepare students in general to meet the complex, mercurial challenges of learning and living in this century. Despite many obstacles, the structures and cultures of U.S. schools can be changed. Beginning with considerations for instructional designs and moving to a reconceptualization of the "place" of school in society, I here discuss implications of our work for increasing the efficacy of teaching and learning—particularly through more effective utilization of digital tools. Assessment of digital learning is also an important issue, but the TEACH Project was not able to significantly address this during the year of this PD work.

Some recent scholars have argued that the design of computer games offers compelling models for other educational and instructional designs. For example, the Federation of American Scientists noted that video games can help reshape education by teaching skills that employers want like analytical thinking, problem solving, multitasking, and team building (Feller 2006). Similarly, Shaffer (2006) noted that epistemic games modeled on the skills used in various professions would be a more viable way to design teaching and learning in schools. Ms. Church's excited statement in the previous section about talk going around the school of a potential collaboration with a new school on the

East Coast alluded to the ideas of modeling on computer designs that were central to the vision of the principal. Instruction in this East Coast school was being completely organized around principles for the design of computer games.

I remember receiving a long e-mail from the principal during the middle of the academic year that exuded his enthusiasm for moving in a similar direction at V-Tech. "For the past two nights I haven't been able to sleep," he wrote. "I came across this school in New York opening in 2009. . . . I want us to create this school on the West coast." He went on to elaborate his sense of the significance of this way of framing schooling.

> This new school has been conceived as a dynamic learning system that takes its cues from the way games are designed, shared and played. This means learning to think about the world as a set of interconnected systems that can be affected or changed through action and choice, the ability to navigate complex information networks, the power to build worlds and tell stories, to see collaboration in competition, and communicate across diverse social spaces. It means that students and teachers will be empowered to innovate using 21st century literacies and engage in their own learning in powerful ways. . . . Imagine a school like this serving our students.

The TEACH Project did not go as far as the vision described by the principal, but some of the implications for redesigns of schooling that linked to our collaborative work did address key considerations in his e-mail. First, in order for students and teachers to be "empowered to innovate using 21st century literacies," the digital technologies that enable these literacies have to be incorporated into instructional designs. This is obvious, of course; yet a fundamental issue addressed in this book was how teachers can gain access to appropriate digital tools in conjunction with how they can best learn to employ them. The project attempted to help teachers see and experience viable ways for new media to be central to their designs for student learning. This required strategies to help some of the teachers get beyond their apprehensions in order to see the use of technology as a resource rather than a threat.

A primary implication from our approach was how the structure for teacher professional development needed to be set up to allow sufficient time and opportunities for teachers to explore and experiment with using digital tools in ways that can help them directly implement their curricular goals. Within the school structure, we created 90-minute bimonthly PD meetings that facilitated caring, collegial relationships as a context for professional development that was seen as relevant to the needs and goals of the teachers. The focus on relationships and relevance was already a part of the school's motto, and the third element of rigor was approached by engaging increasingly complex media, starting with blogs ("If you can do e-mail, you can do a blog," Mr. Cameron told them) and moving to experiences in 3-D virtual environments like Second Life. This process was consistent with the model-building design of learning in Second Life and other digital environments in which the initial structures for learning acted as models for learning other structures that continually increased in complexity and where continual practice was performed en route to competence.

Through the TEACH Project, the participants also experienced how learning with digital tools was "distributed across the learner, objects, tools, symbols, technologies, and the environment" (Gee 2004, 211). In other words, teachers were able to see how their traditional roles as leaders of instruction needed to change to exploit the inherent capabilities of digital media. They could no longer see themselves in relationship to their students like a kind of cue ball in a game of pool, for example, where every animation of student learning had to be initiated by and through the teacher. Students came to be considered as active participants in the learning process, setting some of their own learning goals and experiences. Designs for learning that leverage Gee's distributed principle reflect multiple sites and multimodal ways of learning connected to the material intelligence of the various digital devices. Consequently, new forms of collaboration between and among teachers, students, and the wealth of digital resources were brought into the classrooms. This also suggested the need for redesigning the physical spaces of classrooms, and the use of activity centers provided a good framework in this regard. So the importance of educators coming to appreciate the nature of distributed learning with and through digital tools was another important implication from the work at this school. At the same time, it must be realized that some of the digital tools that we used, like Google applications and Teen Second Life, are privately owned and have commercial purposes that could cause some problems when brought into the context of public schools. Educators will want to think these issues through before building instruction around these particular kinds of tools.

A further implication for instructional design was also revealed in how the teachers engaged in learning in and beyond the PD sessions.

We tried to structure their learning to exemplify ways that the teachers could also design instruction for their students. Aspects of this model have been variously described in this book as "joint productive activity," from CREDE standards; a "pedagogy of collegiality," from Youth Radio principles; or "peer pedagogy," in my own terminology. These approaches to learning move toward being forms of critical pedagogy to the extent that the outcomes and products they create have impacts that help ameliorate inequitable conditions in schooling and ultimately in the world beyond schools. The examples of each of these approaches all revealed the teachers and students collaborating with, modeling for, and learning from each other through production and presentation of and dialogical reflections on digital projects.

This model was seen in the work in our focal classrooms as students' learning took place through project-based activities that often reflected the development of critical perspectives on local and global topics and issues. This occurred, for example, in the blogs, PowerPoint presentations, and podcasts of youth commentaries on topics like racial profiling, post-traumatic stress syndrome, prejudice, and the inequities of institutional power that were developed in Ms. Foster's class. It occurred in the processes of constructing identities, building objects, world traveling, and communicating with others in the virtual world in Ms. Glide's classes. The possibilities for schooling from these kinds of activities were captured in the principal's vision of students developing abilities "to navigate complex information networks" and having "the power to build worlds and tell stories . . . and communicate across diverse social spaces."

Implicit in these new forms of learning was that teachers needed to have a much better understanding of the actual experiences, interests, and skills of the young people in their classrooms in order to create effective instructional designs. Fueled by rapid technological change, youth interests and skills are highly mutable. Consequently, even teachers who are under thirty cannot use their own backgrounds as templates for the digital experiences of contemporary youth, because many of the online social networks and other digital spaces youth currently inhabit barely existed a decade ago. It is estimated that between one-half and three-quarters of U.S. teens have a profile on an Internet social networking site. So a clear implication was that teachers have to work to understand the nature of young people's experiences as they are "hanging out, messing around, and geeking out" with new media (Ito et al. 2009). In their book, Ito and her colleagues synthesized three years of extensive collaborative, ethnographic work from a project funded by the MacArthur Foundation entitled "Kids' Informal Learning with Digital Media." The descriptions draw from a wide range of case studies by a large team of ethnographers to document key "genres of participation"—essential ones being "friendship-driven practices" and "interest-driven practices"—that characterized how young people live and learn through activities that are increasingly mediated digitally.

As our work at V-Tech showed, however, teachers could also use the projects in their classes to gain insights into what their students already know and are able to do with digital media. Teachers were able to design activities to help them better understand the digital intelligence or the digital capital their students possessed. For example, when Terrance was building his virtual presentation space and when DeShawn was building his "world wide wall," they both had photos and music already stored online that they were able to utilize for these class projects. This could happen with traditional class work like essays and other assignments, but an implication from this work was that more modes and mediums were able to be digitally accessed and utilized by students to provide richer and more expansive insights into their experiences and interests. Additionally, the technology offered more extensive and expressive ways for students to share their learning with teachers and other students as well as with communities beyond the school.

V-Tech, in fact, reflected an expanded view of a school's role in the larger community. With the work of students being continually presented beyond their classrooms in community forums, on college campuses, and in online venues, agency and advocacy were given to important issues. The principal consciously worked to make the school function as a viable social unit, and each classroom was also supported to function in the same way. These integral units were focused on the quality of social relationships as the context for engaging in relevant and rigorous learning activities. These were constituent elements of a sense of "place" at V-Tech that was increasingly shared by students, teachers, parents, administrators, staff, and the larger community.

Another implication from the work at V-Tech is that in light of new possibilities for learning with technology, the role of teachers is magnified rather than diminished. Feuerstein et al. (2004) indicated how learning with various tools and materials is significantly extended when a mediator intercedes to systematically modify the learners' interactions and increase their levels of understanding. In these mediations, teachers and students become active, co-constructors of meaning, yet the instruction still guides students in using tools to link their experiences and understandings to new and deeper knowledge. At each level of understanding, teachers must know when and how to release students to more independently internalize and actualize their learning with the various tools.

The TEACH Project brought considerable resources to V-Tech to support the teachers' learning and work to enact new perspectives and use new tools, so aspects of what was achieved might not be immediately reproducible in some educational settings. Yet the descriptions of teaching and learning that occurred at the school indicated the value of instructional designs that utilized unique affordances of new media tools to motivate and facilitate student learning. This learning was active, critical, distributive, multimodal, probing for discovery, and transferable across academic disciplines and social settings. The material intelligence and collective intelligence enabled by the media could also activate a "third participant" and establish a sense of "place" in the process of extending learning into alternative realities. These designs accessed and utilized a significantly wider range of student resources for learning while building on their identities, interests, and culture to expand their understandings of the world. This wider range of resources included an array of multitextual mediums converged in semiotic domains that interrelated and animated actions, images, symbols, and sounds as well as words to make meaning.

Rather than modeling on computer games specifically, the broader implication is for educators to conceive and decide how to implement the emerging possibilities of a wide range of continually changing new media and online resources. New media permeates the lives of young people, and it can bring new life to learning. We must define its place for learning in schools or watch it take the place of schools.

APPENDIX A | THE ISTE NATIONAL EDUCATIONAL TECHNOLOGY STANDARDS AND PERFORMANCE INDICATORS FOR TEACHERS (NETS•T)

Effective teachers model and apply the National Educational Technology Standards for Students (NETS•S) as they design, implement, and assess learning experiences to engage students and improve learning; enrich professional practice; and provide positive models for students, colleagues, and the community. All teachers should meet the following standards and performance indicators. Teachers:

1. Facilitate and Inspire Student Learning and Creativity

Teachers use their knowledge of subject matter, teaching and learning, and technology to facilitate experiences that advance student learning, creativity, and innovation in both face-to-face and virtual environments. Teachers:

a. promote, support, and model creative and innovative thinking and inventiveness

b. engage students in exploring real-world issues and solving authentic problems using digital tools and resources

c. promote student reflection using collaborative tools to reveal and clarify students' conceptual understanding and thinking, planning, and creative processes

d. model collaborative knowledge construction by engaging in learning with students, colleagues, and others in face-to-face and virtual environments

2. Design and Develop Digital-Age Learning Experiences and Assessments

Teachers design, develop, and evaluate authentic learning experiences and assessments incorporating contemporary tools and resources to maximize content learning in context and to develop the knowledge, skills, and attitudes identified in the NETS•S. Teachers:

a. design or adapt relevant learning experiences that incorporate digital tools and resources to promote student learning and creativity

b. develop technology-enriched learning environments that enable all students to pursue their individual curiosities and become active participants in setting their own educational goals, managing their own learning, and assessing their own progress

c. customize and personalize learning activities to address students' diverse learning styles, working strategies, and abilities using digital tools and resources

d. provide students with multiple and varied formative and summative assessments aligned with content and technology standards and use resulting data to inform learning and teaching

3. Model Digital-Age Work and Learning

Teachers exhibit knowledge, skills, and work processes representative of an innovative professional in a global and digital society. Teachers:

a. demonstrate fluency in technology systems and the transfer of current knowledge to new technologies and situations

b. collaborate with students, peers, parents, and community members using digital tools and resources to support student success and innovation

c. communicate relevant information and ideas effectively to students, parents, and peers using a variety of digital-age media and formats

d. model and facilitate effective use of current and emerging digital tools to locate, analyze, evaluate, and use information resources to support research and learning

4. Promote and Model Digital Citizenship and Responsibility

Teachers understand local and global societal issues and responsibilities in an evolving digital culture and exhibit legal and ethical behavior in their professional practices. Teachers:

a. advocate, model, and teach safe, legal, and ethical use of digital information and technology, including respect for copyright, intellectual property, and the appropriate documentation of sources

b. address the diverse needs of all learners by using learner-centered strategies and providing equitable access to appropriate digital tools and resources

c. promote and model digital etiquette and responsible social interactions related to the use of technology and information

d. develop and model cultural understanding and global awareness by engaging with colleagues and students of other cultures using digital-age communication and collaboration tools

5. Engage in Professional Growth and Leadership

Teachers continuously improve their professional practice, model lifelong learning, and exhibit leadership in their school and professional community by promoting and demonstrating the effective use of digital tools and resources. Teachers:

a. participate in local and global learning communities to explore creative applications of technology to improve student learning

b. exhibit leadership by demonstrating a vision of technology infusion, participating in shared decision making and community building, and developing the leadership and technology skills of others

c. evaluate and reflect on current research and professional practice on a regular basis to make effective use of existing and emerging digital tools and resources in support of student learning

d. contribute to the effectiveness, vitality, and self-renewal of the teaching profession and of their school and community

1. Creativity and Innovation

Students demonstrate creative thinking, construct knowledge, and develop innovative products and processes using technology. Students:

   a. apply existing knowledge to generate new ideas, products, or processes
   b. create original works as a means of personal or group expression
   c. use models and simulations to explore complex systems and issues
   d. identify trends and forecast possibilities

2. Communication and Collaboration

Students use digital media and environments to communicate and work collaboratively, including at a distance, to support individual learning and contribute to the learning of others. Students:

   a. interact, collaborate, and publish with peers, experts, or others employing a variety of digital environments and media
   b. communicate information and ideas effectively to multiple audiences using a variety of media and formats
   c. develop cultural understanding and global awareness by engaging with learners of other cultures
   d. contribute to project teams to produce original works or solve problems

3. Research and Information Fluency

Students apply digital tools to gather, evaluate, and use information. Students:

   a. plan strategies to guide inquiry

b. locate, organize, analyze, evaluate, synthesize, and ethically use information from a variety of sources and media

c. evaluate and select information sources and digital tools based on the appropriateness to specific tasks

d. process data and report results

4. Critical Thinking, Problem Solving, and Decision Making

Students use critical thinking skills to plan and conduct research, manage projects, solve problems, and make informed decisions using appropriate digital tools and resources. Students:

a. identify and define authentic problems and significant questions for investigation

b. plan and manage activities to develop a solution or complete a project

c. collect and analyze data to identify solutions and/or make informed decisions

d. use multiple processes and diverse perspectives to explore alternative solutions

5. Digital Citizenship

Students understand human, cultural, and societal issues related to technology and practice legal and ethical behavior. Students:

a. advocate and practice safe, legal, and responsible use of information and technology

b. exhibit a positive attitude toward using technology that supports collaboration, learning, and productivity

c. demonstrate personal responsibility for lifelong learning

d. exhibit leadership for digital citizenship

6. Technology Operations and Concepts

Students demonstrate a sound understanding of technology concepts, systems, and operations. Students:

a. understand and use technology systems

b. select and use applications effectively and productively

c. troubleshoot systems and applications

d. transfer current knowledge to learning of new technologies

NOTES

CHAPTER 1

1. This research collaboration received funding through the Chancellor's Award for Advancing Institutional Excellence at the University of California, Berkeley, and a Corey Grant from the University of California, Berkeley, as well as support from the Digital Youth Project funded by the McArthur Foundation.

2. Village Tech High is a pseudonym for this continuation high school.

3. Pseudonyms are used for all of the teachers and students whose work is discussed in this book and for the school site where the research was conducted.

4. The following are several of the key works that contribute to the discourse on reasons why public schools are failing as well as the limits of numerous reform efforts: Anyon 1997, 2005; Carrol et al. 2004; Cuban 2004; Fruchter 2007; Kozol 1991, 2006; Mickelson 2003; Nieto 2005; Noguera and Wing 2006; Oakes 2005; Ogbu 2003; Witt 2007.

5. See Mahiri 1996, 1998a, 1998b, 2000a, 2000b, 2004a, 2004b, 2006, 2008; Mahiri et al. 2008.

6. Five graduate students, one postdoctoral student, one undergraduate student, and one faculty member in addition to the author were key participants in the TEACH Project from the university during the 2007–8 school year.

7. Five of the teachers who participated were women, and three were men. All except two were under 35 years old. One participant was a Korean woman, and one was a white man. The other six participants were African American. The principal was a 41-year-old, Latino man.

CHAPTER 2

1. The hyphy hip-hop movement began in northern California around 2000 and, in part, is an offshoot of the crunk hip-hop musical style. It is characterized by gritty, thumping sounds and unique dance moves. It also has colorful phrases like "getting hyphy," "getting stupid," and "getting dumb." So when Deja said, "We went stupid," it was a good thing.

REFERENCES

Alvermann, D. E., ed. 2002. *Adolescents and literacies in a digital world.* New York: Peter Lang.

Alvermann, D. E., ed. 2008. *New literacies and digital technologies: A focus on adolescent learners.* New York: Peter Lang.

The American high school: Can it be saved? 2006. *Education Next* 6 (1): 13. Retrieved June 17, 2008, from http://www.hoover.org/publications /ednext/3922606.html.

Anyon, J. 1997. *Ghetto schooling: A political economy of urban educational reform.* New York: Teacher College Press.

Anyon, J. 2005. *Radical possibilities: Public policy, urban education, and a new social movement.* New York: Routledge.

Asimov, N. 2008. 24% likely to drop out at state's high schools. *San Francisco Chronicle,* July 17, A1, A11.

Barab, A., Hay, E., Barnett, M., & Keating, T. 2000. Virtual solar system project: Building understanding through model building. *Journal of Research in Science Teaching* 37 (7): 719–56.

Balfanz, R., and Legters, N. 2004. *Locating the dropout crisis.* Baltimore: Center for Research on the Education of Students Placed At Risk, Johns Hopkins University. Retrieved June 17, 2008, from http://www.csos.jhu.edu/crespar/tech Reports/Report70.pdf.

Barton, D., and Hamilton, M. 2000. Literacy practices. In D. Barton, M. Hamilton, and R. Iranic, eds., *Situated literacies: Reading and writing in context,* 7–15. London: Routledge.

Berry, M. 2008. "Re-embodiment: The dangers and promises of new technologies for learning." Unpublished manuscript, University of California at Berkeley.

Berton, J. 2008. Video blogger Wolf now a real journalist. *San Francisco Chronicle,* August 20, A1, A3. Retrieved September 12, 2008, from http://www.sfgate .com/cgi-bin/article.cgi?f=/c/a/2008/08/20/MNRN129KU4.DTL&hw=Wolf +now+journalist&sn=001&sc=1000.

Bourdieu, P., and Passeron, J. 1977. *Reproduction in education, society, and culture.* Beverly Hills, CA: Sage.

boyd, d. 2007. None of this is real: Identity and participation in Friendster. In J. Karaganis, ed., *Structures of participation in digital culture,* 132–57. New York: Social Science Research Council.

Brooks, D. 2008. Obama, liberalism, and the challenge of reform. *New York Times,* July 27. Retrieved July 27, 2008, from http://www.nytimes.com/2008/06/13 /opinion/13brooks.html.

Bugeja, M. 2007. Second thoughts about second life. *Chronicle of Higher Education* 54 (3): C1.

Callon, M. 1989. Society in the making: The study of technology as a tool for sociological analysis. In W. Bijker et al., eds., *Social construction of technical systems: New directions in the sociology and history of technology,* 83–103. London: MIT Press.

Carey, K. 2007. How low teacher quality sabotages advanced high school math. *Education Sector,* January 8. Retrieved July 21, 2008, from http://www .educationsector.org/analysis/analysis_show.htm?doc_id=440781.

Carroll, T. G., Fulton, K., Abercrombie, K., and Yoon, I. 2004. *Fifty years after Brown v. Board of Education: A two-tiered education system.* Washington, DC: National Commission on Teaching and America's Future.

Charmaraman, L. 2008. Media gangs of social resistance: Urban adolescents take back their images and their streets through media production. *Afterschool Matters* 7:23–33.

Chavez, V., and Soep, E. 2005. Youth Radio and the pedagogy of collegiality. *Harvard Educational Review* 75 (4): 409–34.

Chavez, V., Turalba, R., and Malik, S. 2006. Teaching public health through a pedagogy of collegiality. *American Journal of Public Health* 96 (7): 1175–80.

Chung, A. 2000. *After-school programs: Keeping children safe and smart.* Washington, DC: U.S. Department of Education. Retrieved August 27, 2008, from http://www.ed.gov/pubs/afterschool/index.html.

C. S. Mott Foundation Committee on After-School Research and Practice. 2005. *Moving towards success: Framework for after-school programs.* Washington, DC: Collaborative Communications Group.

Cuban, L. 2004. Why has frequent high school reform since World War II produced disappointing results again, and again, and again? In *The high school reform conference report,* 11–28. New York: MDRC.

Dance, L. J. 2002. *Tough fronts: The impact of street culture on schooling.* New York: RoutledgeFalmer.

Darling-Hammond, L. 1997. *The right to learn: A blueprint for creating schools that work.* San Francisco: Jossey-Bass.

Darling-Hammond, L. 2000. Teacher quality and student achievement: A review of state policy evidence. *Education Policy Archives* 8 (1). Retrieved July 21, 2008, from http://epaa.asu.edu/epaa/v8n1/.

Davis, A. 2005. Co-authoring identity: Digital storytelling in urban middle school. *THEN Journal* 1. Retrieved June 17, 2008, from http://thenjournal .org/feature/61/.

Deleuze, G., and Guattari, F. 1987. *Thousand plateaus: Capitalism and schizophrenia.* Minneapolis: University of Minnesota Press.

Dewey, J. 1938. *Experience and education.* New York: Macmillan.

Doherty, R. W., and Pinal, A. 2004. Joint productive activity and cognitive reading strategy use. *TESOL Quarterly* 38 (3): 219–27.

Douglass, J. A. 2008. Wrong trajectory: America is losing its higher education advantage, with enormous repercussions. *California* 119 (3): 21–23.

Estrada, P., and Imhoff, B. D. 2001. Patterns of language arts instructional activity: Excellence, inclusion, fairness, and harmony in six first grade classrooms. Paper presented at the annual meeting of the American Education Research Association, Seattle, WA.

Feller, B. 2006. Scientist say video games can reshape education. *Utah Daily Herald,* October 17.

Feuerstein, R., Falik, L. H., Feuerstein, R. S., and Rand, Y. 2002. *The dynamic assessment of cognitive modifiability: The learning propensity assessment device; Theory, instruments and techniques.* Jerusalem: ICELP Press.

Feuerstein, R., Falik, L. H., Feuerstein, R. S., and Rand, Y. 2004. *Creating and enhancing cognitive modifiability: Feuerstein's instrumental enrichment program.* Jerusalem: ICELP Press.

Fleetwood, N. R. 2005. Community-based video production and the politics of race and authenticity. *Social Text* 23 (1): 83–109.

Fruchter, N. 2007. *Urban schools, public will: Making education work for all our children.* New York: Teachers College Press.

Gee, J. P. 1990. *Social linguistics and literacies: Ideology in discourses.* London: Farmer Press.

Gee, J. P. 2004. *What video games have to teach us about learning and literacy.* New York: Palgrave Macmillan.

Gibson, W. 2005. God's little toys: Confessions of a cut & paste artist. *Wired,* July, 118–19.

Goodman, S. 2003. *Teaching youth media: A critical guide to literacy, video production, and social change.* New York: Teachers College Press.

Gregory, A., Nygreen, K. and Moran, D. 2006. The discipline gap and the normalization of failure. In P. Noguera and J. Wing, eds., *Unfinished business: Closing the racial achievement gap in our schools,* 121–50. San Francisco: Jossey-Bass.

Gruber, S. 2000. *Weaving a virtual web: Practical approaches to new information technologies.* Urbana, IL: National Council of Teachers of English.

Gutiérrez, K. D. 2002. Studying cultural practices in urban learning communities. *Human Development* 45:312–21.

Haberman, M. 2006. The pedagogy of poverty versus good teaching. *EducationNews,* August 26. Retrieved August 4, 2008, from http://scholar.google.com/scholar?start=10thl=entas_sdt2000+as_vis=1+cluster=140845604.

Halverson, R., and Gomez, L. 1998. Technology and schools: Digital infrastructures think paper metropolitan Chicago group. Retrieved August 25, 2005, from http://www.it.northwestern.edu/metrochicago/think3.htm.

Harrison, S., and Dourish, P. 1996. Re-place-ing space: The roles of place and space in collaborative systems. In *Proceedings of the Conference on Computer-Supported Cooperative Work*, 67–76. New York: Association for Computing Machinery.

Hilberg, R., Chang, J., and Epaloose, G. 2003. *Designing effective activity centers for diverse learners: A guide for teachers at all grade levels and for all subject areas.* Santa Cruz: Center for Research on Education, Diversity, and Excellence, University of California, Santa Cruz.

Hill, M., and Vasudevan, L., eds. 2008. *Media learning and sites of possibility.* New York: Peter Lang.

Horst, H. A., and Miller, D. 2006. *The cell phone: An anthropology of communication.* New York: Berg.

Hull, G., and Katz, M. 2006. Crafting an agentive self: Case studies of digital storytelling. *Research in the Teaching of English* 41 (1): 43–81.

International Society for Technology in Education. 2008. *National Educational Technology Standards for Teachers, 2008.* Retrieved March 19, 2009, from http://www.iste.org/AM/Template.cfm?Section=NETS.

Ito, M. 2007. Technologies of the childhood imagination: *Yu-Gi-Oh!,* Media mixes, and everyday cultural production. In J. Karaganis, ed., *Structures of participation in digital culture,* 86–111. New York: Social Science Research Council.

Ito, M., et al. 2009. *Hanging out, messing around, and geeking out: Kids living and learning with new media.* Cambridge, MA: MIT Press.

Johnson, S. 2005. *Everything bad is good for you: How today's popular culture is actually making us smarter.* New York: Riverhead Books.

Kitwana, B. 2002. *The hip hop generation: Young blacks and the crisis in African-American culture.* New York: Basic Civitas Books.

Kozol, J. 1991. *Savage inequalities: Children in America's schools.* New York: Harper Perennial.

Kozol, J. 2006. *The shame of the nation: The restoration of apartheid schooling in America.* New York: Three Rivers.

Laird, J., DeBell, M., Kienzl, G., and Chapman, C. 2007. *Dropout rates in the United States: 2005.* NCES 2007-059. Washington, DC: National Center for Education Statistics. Retrieved June 17, 2008, from http://nces.ed.gov/pubsearch.

Lakoff, G. 2004. *Don't think of an elephant: Know your values and frame the debate.* White River Junction, VT: Chelsea Green.

Lankshear, C., and Knobel, M. 2002. Do we have your attention? New literacies, digital technologies, and the education of adolescents. In D. E. Alvermann, ed., *Adolescents and literacies in a digital world,* 19–39. New York: Peter Lang.

Latour, B. 2005. *Reassembling the social: An Introduction to Actor-Network-Theory.* Oxford: Oxford University Press.

Lave, J. 1988. *Cognition in practice: Mind, mathematics, and culture in everyday life.* Cambridge: Cambridge University Press.

Law, J., and Hassard, J., eds. 1999. *Actor network theory and after.* Oxford: Blackwell; Keele: Sociological Review.

Lee, C. D. 2005. Taking culture into account: Intervention research based on current views of cognition and learning. In J. King, ed., *Black education: A transformative research and action agenda for the new century*, 73–114. Mahwah, NJ: Lawrence Erlbaum Associates.

Linn, M., and Davis, E. 2004. *Internet environments for science education*. Mahwah, NJ: Lawrence Erlbaum Associates.

Linn, M., and Hsi, S. 2000. *Computers, teachers, peers: Science learning partners*. Mahwah, NJ: Lawrence Erlbaum Associates.

Luke, A. 1998. Getting over method: Literacy teaching as work in "new times." *Language Arts* 75 (4): 305–13.

Mahiri, J. 1996. Clicking on an icon: How technology helped amplify the "microvoices" of student writers. *Quarterly of the National Writing Project and the Center for the Study of Writing and Literacy* 18 (3): 1–8.

Mahiri, J. 1998a. *Shooting for excellence: African American and youth culture in new century schools*. New York: Teachers College Press; Urbana, IL: National Council of Teachers of English.

Mahiri, J. 1998b. Streets to schools: African American youth culture in the classroom. *Clearing House* 71 (6): 335–39.

Mahiri, J. 2000a. Pop culture pedagogy and the ends(s) of school. *Journal of Adolescent and Adult Literacy* 44 (4): 382–86.

Mahiri, J. 2000b. What will the social implications and interactions of schooling be in the next millennium? *Reading Research Quarterly* 35 (3): 420–25.

Mahiri, J. 2004a. New teachers for new times: The dialogical principle in teaching and learning electronically. In S. Freedman and A. Ball, eds., *Bakhtinian perspectives on language, literacy, and learning*, 213–31. Cambridge: Cambridge University Press.

Mahiri, J., ed. 2004b. *What they don't learn in school: Literacy in the lives of urban youth*. New York: Peter Lang.

Mahiri, J. 2006. Digital DJ-ing: Rhythms of learning in an urban school. *Language Arts* 84 (1): 55–62.

Mahiri, J. 2008. New literacies need new learning. A professional development wiki for educators, developed for the Improving Teacher Quality Project (ITQP), a federally funded partnership between Montclair State University and East Orange School District, New Jersey. Available at http://www.newlits.wikispaces.com/Digi-Pop+-+New+Literacies+Needs+New+Learning.

Mahiri, J., and Conner, E. 2003. Black youth violence has a bad rap. *Journal of Social Issues* 59 (1): 121–40.

Mahiri, J., Ali, M., Scott, A., Asmerom, B., and Ayers, R. 2008. Both sides of the mic: Community literacies in the age of hip hop. In J. Flood, S. B. Heath, and D. Lapp, eds., *Research on teaching literacy through the communicative, visual, and performing arts*, 2: 279–87. Mahwah, NJ: Lawrence Erlbaum Associates.

Manovich, L. 2001. *The language of new media*. Cambridge, MA: MIT Press.

McLaren, P., Hammer, R., Sholle, D., and Reilly, S., eds. 1995. *Rethinking media literacy: A critical pedagogy of representation*. New York: Peter Lang.

McNeil, L. M., Coppola, E., Radigan, J., and Vasquez Heilig, J. 2008. Avoidable losses: High-stakes accountability and the dropout crisis. *Education Policy Analysis Archives* 16 (3). Retrieved June 17, 2008, from http://epaa.asu.edu /epaa/v16n3/.

Mickelson, R. A. 2003. When are racial disparities in education the result of racial discrimination? A social science perspective. *Teachers College Record* 105(6): 1052–86.

Miller, P. 2004. *Rhythm science*. Cambridge, MA: MIT Press.

Nieto, S. 2005. Public education in the twentieth century and beyond: High hopes, broken promises, and an uncertain future. *Harvard Educational Review* 75 (1): 43–64.

Noddings, N. 2006. *Critical lessons: What our schools should teach*. New York: Cambridge University Press.

Noguera, P. 1995. Preventing and producing violence: A critical analysis of responses to school violence. *Harvard Educational Review* 65 (2): 189–212.

Noguera, P. 2003. *City schools and the American Dream: Reclaiming the promise of public education*. New York: Teachers College Press.

Noguera, P., and Wing, J. Y. 2006. *Unfinished business: Closing the racial achievement gap in our schools*. San Francisco: Jossey-Bass.

Oakes, J. 2005. *Keeping track: How schools structure inequality*. New Haven, CT: Yale University Press.

Ogbu, J. U. 2003. *Black American students in an affluent suburb: A study of academic disengagement*. Mahwah, NJ: Lawrence Erlbaum Associates.

Pea, R. 1993. Practices of distributed intelligence and designs for education. In G. Salomon, ed., *Distributed cognitions: Psychological and educational considerations*, 47–87. New York: Cambridge University Press.

Poyntz, S. R. 2006. Independent media, youth agency, and the promise of media education. *Canadian Journal of Education* 29 (1): 154–75.

Rich, M. 2008. Literacy debate: Online, R U really reading? *New York Times*, July 27. Retrieved July 28, 2008, from http://www.nytimes.com/2008/07/27 /books/27reading.html.

Rose, T. 1994. Black noise: Rap music and black culture in contemporary America. Middletown, CT: Wesleyan University Press.

Salomon, G., ed. 1993. *Distributed cognitions: Psychological and educational considerations*. New York: Cambridge University Press.

Saunders, W., and Goldenberg, C. 1999. The effects of instructional conversations on English proficient students. Research report 6. Center for Research on Education, Diversity, and Excellence, University of California, Santa Cruz.

Saunders, W., O'Brien, G., Lennon, D., and McLean, J. 1998. Making the transition to English literacy successful: Effective strategies for studying literature with transition students. In R. G. R. Jimenez, ed., *Promoting learning for culturally and linguistically diverse students*, 79–94. Monterey, CA: Brooks Cole.

Shaffer, D. W. 2006. *How computer games help children learn.* New York: Palgrave Macmillan.

Shaffer, D. W., Squire, K., Halverson, R., and Gee, J. 2005. Video games and the future of learning. *Phi Delta Kappan* 87 (2): 104–11.

Sholle, D., and Denski, S. 1993. Reading and writing the media: Critical media literacy and postmodernism. In C. Lankshear and P. McLaren, eds., *Critical literacy: Politics, praxis, and the postmodern,* 297–321. New York: State University of New York Press.

Soep, E. 2006. Beyond literacy and voice in youth media production. *McGill Journal of Education* 41 (3): 197–213.

Spencer, M. B. 2008. Lessons learned and opportunities ignored since *Brown v. Board of Education*: Youth development and the myth of a color-blind society. *Educational Researcher* 37 (5): 253–66.

Stigler, J. W., and Hiebert, J. 1999. *The teaching gap: Best ideas from the world's teachers for improving education in the classroom.* New York: Free Press.

Stoddart, T. 1999. Language acquisition through science inquiry. Paper presented at the annual meeting of the American Education Research Association, Montreal.

Stoddart, T. 2005. Improving student achievement with the CREDE five standards pedagogy. Technical report, no. J1. Center for Research on Education, Diversity and Excellence, University of California, Santa Cruz.

Street, B. 1984. *Literacy in theory and practice.* Cambridge: Cambridge University Press.

Tharp, R. G., Estrada, P., Dalton, S. S., and Yamauchi, L. A. 2001. *Teaching transformed: Achieving excellence, fairness, inclusion, and harmony.* Boulder, CO: Westview.

Tompkins, G. E. 2006. *Literacy for the 21st century: A balanced approach.* Upper Saddle River, NJ: Pearson Merrill Prentice Hall.

Vygotsky, L. S. 1978. *Mind in society: Development of higher psychological processes.* Cambridge: Harvard University Press.

Warschauer, M. 2006. *Laptops and literacy: Learning in the wireless classroom.* New York: Teachers College Press.

Willoughby, T., and Wood, E., eds. 2008. *Children's learning in a digital world.* Malden, MA: Blackwell.

Witt, H. 2007. School discipline tougher on African Americans. *Chicago Tribune,* September 25. Retrieved June 17, 2008, from http://www.chicagotribune.com/services/newspaper/printedition/tuesday/chi-070924discipline,0,5751354.story?page=2.

INDEX

Page numbers followed by letter *f* refer to figures.